Your Pursuit of Profit

YOUR PURSUIT OF PROFIT

How to Motivate Yourself and Others for
Business and Personal Success

Christine Harvey
with
Bill Sykes

**KOGAN
PAGE**

Dedication

To all the friends, family, associates, clients, consultants, who made
this possible

First published in 1986 by Sphere as *In Pursuit of Profit*.
This revised edition published in 1988 by
Kogan Page Ltd, 120 Pentonville Road, London N1 9JN

Typeset by DP Photosetting, Aylesbury, Bucks
Printed and bound in Great Britain by
Billings & Sons Ltd, Worcester

British Library Cataloguing in Publication Data

Harvey, Christine
    Your pursuit of profit. – Rev. ed.
    1. Salesmanship – Manuals
    I. Title   II. Sykes, Bill   III. Harvey,
    Christine. In pursuit of profit
    658.8'5

    ISBN 1-85091-771-X
    ISBN 1-85091-770-1 Pbk

Contents

Press Comments

WEALTH MAGAZINE—LONDON

'A masterpiece of presentation selling.'

SUNDAY STANDARD—HONGKONG

'One woman who has caught the gut essence of what it takes to stay at the top *is Christine Harvey, co-author of the best selling* Your Pursuit of Profit, *she teaches us that "motivational psychology" is the name of the game.'*

EXPORT DIRECTION—LONDON

'Examples on every page' *'certainly recommended.'*

BAWE BUSINESS NEWS—LONDON

'With 9000 copies sold the first month, Your Pursuit of Profit *stems from the authors' insight of seeing the same pitfalls repeating themselves again and again—and advises aptly on how to change it.'*

BRITISH INSTITUTE OF MANAGEMENT MAGAZINE— LONDON

'Statistics prove that 75% of all potential new business is lost on the customer's first contact' ... *Find the reasons in* Your Pursuit of Profit.

AUSTRALIAN INSTITUTE OF MANAGEMENT—SYDNEY

Your Pursuit of Profit
'The motivation business book that has broken sales records in the UK and abroad, is now published in 6 languages—English, French, Dutch, German, Swedish and Japanese ... and now American and Australian editions.'

TRENDS—BELGIUM

At last, this book gives 'structure to selling on a high level.'

BIRMINGHAM POST—BIRMINGHAM

Author Mrs. Christine Harvey ... 'is a human dynamo jetting across the world—she dismisses the notion that the ideal salesman is a smooth talking, super-confident operator!'

TOKYO BUSINESS TODAY—JAPAN

'Your Pursuit of Profit *teaches that the point where the employees' goal and the company's goal intersect, is the point of motivation.'*

DE FINANCIEEL ECONOMISCHE TIJO—BELGIUM

'80% of sales people are putting their effort in at the wrong time.'

THE STAR—MALAYSIA

'Your Pursuit of Profit *can just as easily be "Your Search of $$$Happiness".'*

INTERMEDIAIR—BELGIUM

'... Your Pursuit of Profit, *a book that is really making the blitz in management and business circles....'*

DE STANDAARD—BELGIUM

We learn that 'Money is only the third highest motivation,' from Your Pursuit of Profit.

NEW STRAITS TIMES—KUALA LUMPUR

Author Christine Harvey: she is 'The guru of profit-making.'

PEAK MAGAZINE—HONGKONG

'The book looks poised to take over some of it's best known predecessors, such as The One-Minute Manager *and* In Search of Excellence.'

About the Authors

Christine Harvey

An award-winning sales executive in her own right, Christine Harvey has been running her own consulting and sales training company, Intrinsic Marketing, since 1980. A shining example of someone able to combine business and personal success, she has been described by colleagues as 'a person who accomplishes everything she sets out to do' and by the press as 'the guru of profit and personal motivation.'

Her unique approach to consulting and training has assisted companies from here and abroad to dramatically increase sales. Her work takes her throughout the USA, Europe, the Middle East, and the Far East. In addition, she is a popular guest on television, and a motivational speaker at conferences and public and in-house seminars.

Mrs Harvey brings diverse and wide-reaching experiences to her speaking, writing, and consulting. This helps her to relate the successes of people in different industries to each other. As an entrepreneur, she has founded three businesses of her own. Her corporate expertise in sales, marketing, and management was gained from AT&T and from the highly competitive fields of advertising and computing, as well as property, retailing, and consulting worldwide.

She was the 1987–88 Chairman of the London Commerce and Industry West Section, the first woman to hold that position. She is also on the Board of Directors of an Enterprise Agency launched by Prince Charles which provides consultation and assistance to start up companies in England. She founded 'The Most Promising Young Business Woman Award' in 1980 to help women progress faster in making significant contributions to industry. Awarded annually to a university age woman, it is comprised of a cash award, specially selected training, and ongoing support.

An American educated at UCLA, Christine has been a resident of England since 1976. She lives with her husband, Tom, near London.

They have three adult children, Laurie, Darrin, and Tom, launching their own careers in America following their English education.

Bill Sykes

As Principal of Sykes Consultants, which specializes in organizational development, Bill Sykes uses his marketing and organizational skills to help companies increase their results. He is described as 'a person whose undying enthusiasm makes him a valued colleague' and by his clients as having 'a unique ability to bring people together constructively to enhance the results of all concerned.'

His consulting work with his own firm, and collaboration with Intrinsic Marketing, employs his ability to get things done through people. His clients in organization development include professional partnerships and industrial and consumer companies. With Intrinsic Marketing, he assists clients to export through setting up opportunities with buyers and agents overseas. Along with Christine Harvey, he has founded the highly successful 'Pursuit of Profit' Seminars for personal and company development, now run in Tokyo, Singapore, Brussels, London, Athens, and throughout America.

Prior to his entrepreneurial activities, Mr Sykes gained corporate experience in marketing and human resources at Horlicks Pharmaceuticals and with the Beecham group. Later, with Black and Decker, he held the position of Corporate Director of Personnel based in the USA with previous responsibility for their Pacific International Operations. His expertise in overseas business took him to the Far East, North and South America, and Europe.

He is active in educational and community affairs and has particular interest in counselling executives. His expertise in personality profiles as they relate to organizational development and to fulfilment on and off the job brings him to addressing community and seminar groups.

Bill is British, and was educated at Sedbergh in England before gaining a Master's degree in Business Studies. He has resided in America since 1976 on both the East and West Coasts and lives with his wife, Angela, and their two sons, James and Charles, in a picturesque, wooded suburb of Baltimore near Washington, DC.

Preface
How—and Why—
This Book Was Written

Doesn't everyone in the world have a message to get across? Of course
they do. We all find ourselves wanting to ask for higher pay or
promotions, or wanting to convince our spouse, our children, our
colleagues of something—day in and day out. Yet, how many of us have
been trained to get our message across effectively?

When I was at school, I was taught that the road to success was
through knowledge. When I was in my teens, I started to question this
'fact.'

I looked at the successful people around me, and it was clear that they
were people who could motivate others. They were people who could
get their ideas across effectively. They were not necessarily the ones with
the most education, or even the ones with the best ideas. This worried
me. I became less convinced that education was the road to success and
more fascinated with the concept of putting ideas across.

At that stage I didn't link the concept of putting ideas across with the
sales process. I was concerned only with how I could acquire this skill.
I was sure education *alone* would not bring me what I wanted in life—
either personally or professionally. Also, I wondered about the running
of corporations. If my premise was right, many people with excellent
ideas and education were not making their points heard and were
therefore not influencing decisions. Good *potential* leadership was
being overlooked.

From that moment on, regardless of where I was, I became a keen
observer of the way people put their ideas across. Frequently at
important meetings, I saw others wait until the meeting was over to
express their ideas. Often these ideas were better than the ones brought
out during the meeting. Many times I found myself in the same position.
I became more and more convinced that the world needs input from

everyone to improve conditions. 'But what can one person do?' I thought.

So I decided to keep watching and learning. I took every opportunity to look, listen, and learn from successful people. Each job added a principle to the new formula I was developing from my experience. Before long, the principles started to fit together like an equation in algebra. Instead of mystique, there seemed to be logic. I saw that people used certain specific methods to get their message across—to influence and motivate others.

But I still didn't link the methods with sales. To me, 'sales' was something people did in retail stores. I started to use the principles and get results. I knew that they were helping me to easily achieve things I wanted in life.

For example, despite the fact that there were three unemployed teachers for every employed teacher, I used the principles to get a teaching position, even though I had no previous experience. I used them later to get a job in a very competitive area of advertising, and still later to break into the computer field. Eventually these principles proved to be invaluable in starting my own business, where I enjoyed a wide range of activities while motivating others. I continued to watch other people use the principles to develop their lives.

But the methods made the greatest impact on me when I used them in teaching, before I went into business. The school principal called me into his office to tell me that I was being assigned 'a group of low-achieving troublemakers.' You can imagine the terror that struck me as a new teacher. 'How will I motivate them?' I asked myself.

I decided to use my formula. That would be the real test. I decided to 'sell' the students on the idea of achievement.

It worked. Several teachers commented on the students' performance to me. One asked, 'What's been happening to those students? I've never seen them care about learning before. Today I even saw some of them studying for your exam during *my* class!'

At the end of the semester, even I was amazed to find that the six worst school troublemakers were, without exception, all high achievers. So were the others in that class.

I hadn't taught them anything. I'd simply helped them to motivate themselves. I'd helped them channel their energy into achievement. When they learned that achievement was possible, they started their own upward spiral. It kept going and it fed on itself. It was more self-rewarding than their previous downward spiral. That one year's experience taught me more about motivation and selling than any single experience I have had. It taught me that motivating others by getting messages across is a basic human necessity.

We all have wants and needs that must be met. The better we can express these *and* find out the needs of others, the better we can create solutions that improve the quality of our lives.

And that's selling: finding out the needs of others, getting a message across about what we have to offer, and then fulfilling their needs by coming to an amicable conclusion.

It was in 1983 that Bill Sykes and I met and brought our philosophies together. Bill had been running his own consultancy in America and I had been running mine in Britain for some time. Since Bill was British and living in America, and I was American and living in Britain, we saw similar problems and opportunities that companies face in selling across international borders.

Bill and I were introduced to each other by one of the advisers at the Institute of Directors in London. They knew what I was doing in sales training and export assistance, and they knew what Bill was doing with companies on organizational development. They thought Bill could assist us with clients that wanted to develop sales outlets or licensing relationships in the USA, and vice versa.

From the beginning, Bill and I have looked closely at the needs of companies in their business development. What makes them fail? What helps them succeed? Just as the principles of successful people formed a pattern, so did those of successful businesses. Certain patterns ran through large and small companies, regardless of their business. Some were manufacturers. Some were service companies. Some were professional groups. We wanted to spread the word about the successes so that the patterns could be adopted by all companies and modified to their needs. It seems pointless to re-invent the wheel when workable principles already exist.

The result was the development of an intensive seminar to show all directors and executives how to sell and how to get their ideas across. We addressed not only the people in sales—we addressed everyone who could influence sales. Since 75% of all business is lost on first contact with a company, we knew everyone affects sales—service, finance, production—they all play a part. Their ability to motivate people and to get their message across dramatically affects company performance.

In the following pages you'll see examples of ways people have used these principles in their lives and their businesses. You'll see people who have dramatically increased their business against all odds, people who have gained positions of leadership and community recognition, people whose valuable ideas are influencing others. You'll see the same principles being used successfully in the USA, England, Japan, Canada, and Australia—around the globe.

The purpose of this book is to give you the basic principles that apply to increasing sales in domestic and overseas markets. *The principles will help you to get the results you want, no matter where you are or what you do in life.* The examples have been chosen to give you insight and the inspiration to push the principles into action. They'll help you to increase sales and increase enjoyment in life and business by positioning your company, your product, or your ideas in the most effective way.

The principles described in this book are not theoretical, untested concepts. They are practical, tried and tested practices that work for large companies, small companies, or individuals. They are practices that can be used to obtain immediate results.

The course members on our seminars who learn the principles are usually amazed at how quickly they get results. Some call and tell us they've made cassettes to listen to while they drive to work to remind them of the principles and how to use them. One director of a pharmaceutical company told us that he picks out a new principle regularly to work on. Gradually the principles become incorporated into his management practices. 'One of the principles, the one on using benefits,' he said, brought him 'a 25% increase in sales in the first three months.'

He gave us the credit for the principles, but he earned all the credit for carrying them out. After all, as Samuel Johnson said, 'To do nothing is in every man's power.' That was in the 1750s. It's still true today. Yet the achievers, I'm discovering over and over again, are those who follow a very simple two-step process. The first is to *decide* exactly what they want. The second is to *do* it.

The world needs input from us all. We all want to be in charge of our own lives, and to create success for ourselves as *we* see it. Christopher Morley summed it up nicely by saying, 'There is only one success—to be able to spend your life in your own way.' That takes self-determination. It takes skill in understanding ourselves and others. It takes practice in setting and reaching our goals—in motivating ourselves and others to reach those goals.

Our aim is to get the best ideas and principles into circulation for the good of all. This will help people achieve the maximum potential for themselves, their company, their family, and their community. If you glean one concept from this book that you put into *action*, then this book will have achieved its goal. For an idea or principle not put into circulation serves no one. We wish you good luck in achieving your own success.

Christine Harvey
65 Blandford Street
London

In collaboration with

Bill Sykes
400 East Pratt Street
Baltimore

Introduction

Shortly after this book was first released, in 1986, I had a speaking tour in the Far East.

During the tour I stopped in Tokyo, and took a weekend trip up to Lake Ashi, a tranquil mountain resort only an hour or so from Tokyo, by the bullet train and taxi. Mr Morita, the Chairman of Sony, and other Japanese executives have weekend homes there.

As I stood at the hotel room over looking the beautiful snowcapped mountains, I decided to delve into *The Teachings of Buddha*, which laid on the bedside table, while I waited for dinner.

Something told me I'd find a marketing story in it, and believe it or not, I did find one within the first 15 pages.

The story tells of a father who comes home at night and finds his house burning down. He's frantic because his children are inside and he calls in, 'Children, children, quick come out, the house is burning down.'

The children are busy playing and pay no attention.

The father thinks again, 'What can I do?'

Suddenly he gets a brilliant idea and calls in again, 'Children, children, quick come out, I have a present for you.'

This time the children's ears perk up and they hear the word 'present'. Present *means* something to them and they come running out.

It's not that the house burning down was not important. It was important to the father. But the children didn't understand the significance to them. They didn't care, so they didn't act.

As I read the story, I thought how often in life—personal and business—we talk in terms of our own interest, not the interest of the other people we're trying to motivate or sell to.

No wonder we don't always get the results we want.

In our seminars I started telling people to remember the Buddha story. To visualize a house burning down to remind them to put the 'present' forward to people rather than the 'house burning down'.

This applies to sales visits, telephone calls, management meetings, wording of literature, etc; every aspect of life when we want to motivate people. When we show that *their* objectives match our ability to supply, we succeed.

Different people throughout the world have used the principles of this book and our seminars in various ways to get phenomenal results. One woman in Belgium who heads a chemical company there and in Holland, went back to rewrite her technical data sheets to include the benefits of each sheet. She reasoned that if people could understand the benefit first, they would absorb the technical data better. It worked.

But she didn't stop there. She also decided to take 10 minutes out of her busy day to talk to each of her salesman to find out what *they* wanted from their job—challenge, variety, learning, working with new people and so on.

She achieved a 140% increase in revenue in 12 months. She got it by emphasizing benefits with people and products.

Another person took the area of targets, and increased his business by 40% in three months. He did this at our suggestion, by simply changing his sales team over from monthly to weekly targets.

Another person also had a 40% increase, this time in two months after reading the book. He chose to implement an airtight follow-up system for his leads. Often people lose potential business needlessly because they start a lot of sales activities, but don't have an effective easy system for reminding them what needs following up. Therefore they abandon their efforts midstream, and their previous energy is wasted.

The answer to all this is simplicity.

I had a call from one of my training consultants recently, and he said, 'Christine, have you seen Tom Peter's new book?' There was a sound of urgency in his voice.

'No, why?' I asked.

'He's copied your ideas,' he said. 'I went to one of his lectures and his ideas are the same as yours.'

'Which ones are those?' I asked.

'Well, getting back to basics. Getting the core right. Not putting in superficial solutions which gloss over the problem.'

'Yes, that sounds like me,' I said, 'And like the movement in management lately worldwide.'

The point is that people are tired of pie-in-the-sky solutions. The days of theoretical solutions which need a mental translation before they can be applied, are gone.

In this fast moving world people want flexible, basic solutions. They want to be able to apply it *now* for results.

I believe in a 100% philosophy. Go for small change and big results. You can't turn your current systems upside down. That's not practical. *But*, if you can make a *10% change to get 100% better results*, that's practical, that's worth it.

In this book and in our seminars, we help you look for that 10% change to get 100% and upwards better results.

We show you the experiences of others.

You probably have a good system now. But, if you could finetune it 10% to get 100% better results, wouldn't it be worth it?

I'll always remember the impact that the words of Dr Morehouse had on me. Dr Morehouse was a trainer for the US Olympic champions. He said you can practice all you want, but if you are practising wrong, you'll never get better!

Think of how that applies to your own systems. If you are practising it wrong, you'll never get better results.

In athletics it's often just a 10% change in the way you let your foot touch the ground that makes the difference between medium and high performance.

In factories, such as textiles, where productivity is important, machinists are taught to reduce their hand and arm movements in order to get better results. The change in movements is slight, but the change in results is dramatic.

In managing ourselves and our company, we can do the same thing. Changing from monthly to weekly or daily targets is a slight change— but the results are dramatic.

Changing from talking about the features of our product or service to talking about the benefits, is a slight change. But the results are dramatic.

Finally, if you want to make a dramatic change in your results my suggestion is to choose a few principles in this book and actually *use* them. Don't just agree with them.

To know something is not enough. It's the use of the skill that counts.

We've supplied action sheets for you at the end of each section, on which you can write your ideas down as they occur to you. You then have a referral sheet for action.

It's said that it takes one month to form a habit and two weeks to break it. By using the principles, they will become habit.

It's been tremendously rewarding to Bill Sykes and me to have letters from readers from all parts of the world telling us how they've used the principles.

The book is now published in French, German, Dutch, Swedish, Japanese and has American and Australian editions as well.

We'll be very pleased to hear how you implement the principles for results and if you still want more practice, call us. We'll come out to do an intensive seminar with your group. Practice, of the right kind, makes perfect.

After all, if you want results you might as well do it right as to do it wrong. It requires the same amount of energy, often less. Bon voyage!

Fundamental Facts
You Should Know
About Sales

1

Maximize the Contribution—of Ourselves and Others

A talented young woman named Margo Ross landed a job in the heart of London's financial district. The company is one of the world's most prestigious. Margo was hired because of her outstanding academic record and because she expressed herself well during the interviews. Her job would be to assess business proposals and to make lending decisions—a responsible position, indeed.

After six months the company was impressed with her performance. They saw her learning fast, communicating well with clients. She was able to make clear-cut decisions and so they earmarked her for a senior management position in the investment division.

From the first week in her management position, Margo found herself sitting in meetings in the company's palatial boardroom. 'I freeze up at those meetings', she said. 'The others are so much more experienced than I am. I just feel so inadequate.' Despite her talent and well-founded ideas, she is unable to express herself at the meetings. She has good ideas, but she hesitates to put herself forward.

She told me about her concern. 'Christine, I know it's silly,' she said, 'but what if I say the wrong thing? Surely they've thought about everything I've thought of anyway.'

Fortunately, her manager is patient and supportive, hoping that as she becomes more comfortable with her new environment she will contribute more freely. She will move into the management shoes.

This woman is lucky. Most of us don't operate in an atmosphere which waits for us to catch up. Usually there is someone else there, ready to move into our shoes if we hesitate and falter. But even for Margo, her chances for success are linked to the speed she moves toward contributing to her new environment.

Why did Margo feel confident in one work situation and helpless in another? Her predicament is similar to ones we all face in our lives.

People have certain situations in which they operate comfortably, but when the threshold of challenge becomes too high, they hesitate.

What will happen to Margo if she doesn't live up to management expectations as time goes on? Chances are that she'll lose further promotions, and her opportunity to contribute to the company. When that happens, she'll lose her self esteem and her chance for self development. That won't help her or her company.

Conquer challenges at each threshold

What holds Margo back? Or, for that matter, what holds any of us back? We all know from past experience that we feel best about ourselves when we're reaching new heights and accomplishing new goals.

Emerson summed up the reason quite nicely when he said, 'Fear defeats more people than any one single thing in the world.'

No wonder Margo is afraid to get up in the boardroom among people far senior to herself. She's in good company. It's said that 'People are more afraid of getting up on their feet to speak in public than of dying!' When it comes to expressing themselves in a challenging environment fear looms over the heads of most people—unless they learn to conquer it.

Margo's at a turning point in her life. Will she take action to accept the challenge for self development and leadership now while the opportunity presents itself? Or will she kid herself into thinking that her skill and confidence will develop if she sits back without accepting the new challenge? The answer is in her hands.

I know Margo and I know she'll meet her challenges head on. Her drive and determination will help her to overcome her hesitation. But for every person like Margo there are many others who won't—not without assistance and motivation.

When we look at people who achieve the greatest success in their fields, we see that they are constantly pushing their challenge threshold to new heights. They bite off one bit of the challenge, conquer it, and move on to the next. They keep pushing that challenge threshold further and further along. In the process they gain invaluable practice, experience, and skill which helps them bite off new challenges and achieve new heights.

It's people like this that we need when we pursue profit. But they are not lurking in every doorway waiting to be hired. They have to be developed. When we develop others, our profit potential soars as each person and their contribution goes from strength to strength.

Advance your goals and self image

I heard it said once, many years ago, that 'Our happiness is directly linked to the speed at which we're moving towards our goal.' Think of it! The faster we're moving towards our goal, the happier we are. But surely we can't move towards our goal if we let fear stop us!

It is said that '60% of our self image is based on the job we have'. Sixty percent! That means our job is responsible for more than half of our self image. What will happen to Margo's self image if she ends up with a job which is beneath her real potential? Her confidence will go down, and her ability to contribute will lessen.

If she decides to conquer each new challenge, her skills will increase, she'll continue to progress and her image will strengthen. She'll be a happier person and a better catalyst to others in their development.

And so it goes in business, and even in personal life. Some people seem to excel at accepting challenges and increasing their contribution—while others hesitate. And the pattern can become set. The achievers continue to achieve and the hesitators continue to hesitate—unless they change their pattern.

Influence others to develop patterns of highest achievement

The real question for all of us who are determined to pursue profit is how to influence this pattern. Everyone reading this book already has the conviction necessary to succeed or you wouldn't be interested in this subject. Yet we all need to motivate others in order to reach the highest goals. And when it comes to ourselves, we know we too can achieve higher goals—we can push our own challenge threshold along with greater speed and greater satisfaction.

The question is how to keep others and ourselves moving through the challenge thresholds. Why not take a leaf out of the book of the most successful?

Isn't life too short to re-invent the wheel each time we set out to do things? Surely we can advance faster if we take the best methods and adapt them to our own needs.

That's exactly why we've written this book. To bring people the best methods of the successful, which can be adapted quickly and effectively, for maximum results.

The results apply to business for those pursuing profit and to the community and personal life for the profit of all concerned. For it is only when people function at their best that we all stand to profit—only then do we get the best ideas and the best decisions.

Acknowledge strengths and weaknesses

One of my goals in life is to get young people with high ability and high moral values contributing to business to their maximum capability. I want to see the best brains, and the best talents, making an impact on society.

At my company, Intrinsic Marketing, I take management trainees from various parts of the world. They come for work experience during their college years or just after graduation and stay for a fixed period.

During that time I use a method which makes their confidence and skill rise enormously. I have them carry a small notebook to record two things they *like* doing, and things they *feel satisfaction* from in terms of their contribution or achievement. They must record two things every day.

What do you think happens? Without exception, regardless of where they come from, they are unable at first to acknowledge the good things. They're embarrassed or they get so burderned down with their inabilities that they can't, at first, think of good points. But we persist.

After a week of recording two things a day, they have 10 things they're good at or enjoy. After a month, they have 40. A trend starts to develop.

They see things about themselves that they never knew. We see things about them we wouldn't otherwise know. Their self esteem goes up. So does their contribution.

They look at their strengths and weaknesses honestly and openly. They try to improve their weaknesses and ride on their strengths.

Soon they talk on the phone, and in person, to presidents of our client companies around the world. They love the challenges.

They soon learn to tackle high-level responsibilities. After they leave, they write to say how extraordinarily their confidence has gone up and their goals have changed.

Now there are five years' worth of past trainees, and among them is hardly one who doesn't still write to keep us informed of their progress and to tell us of the impact their traineeship had, as they continue to go from strength to strength.

In the course of life we meet many types of people. Not all are successful. Unfortunately, many haven't learned to be as honest with themselves about their strengths and weaknesses as the trainees have. They spend more time covering up the weaknesses than improving the strengths. They haven't realized they can't be all things to all people. In trying to do that, they destroy their own confidence.

Their lack of understanding about themselves prevents them from doing their best. What a shame. There are such talented people held back by their own lack of understanding of themselves. If we are to motivate others, we have to understand ourselves first.

People are a little like businesses. If we don't identify the problem, we can't cure it. If we don't identify the strength, we can't make best use of it.

Do it now

I remember one evening sitting with my husband watching the story of Gilbert and Sullivan on television. In one scene Sullivan was in the south of France having a well-deserved rest. The wife of his business manager arrived to extend an invitation from England to him to write two new operas. What did Sullivan do?

Upon hearing the news, he jumped out of his chair in the middle of the hotel lounge, ready to rush of to England. The woman who brought him the news had to restrain him to finish his coffee before jolting off, his enthusiasm and eagerness to 'do it now' was so great.

With this attitude, is there any wonder that his works became known around the world?

A client of mine, Julia Davies, had a superb sign in her office at Horsell Graphic. It said, 'Do it today, for tomorrow it will take twice as long, and next week three times as long'. What's worse, as you and I know, leaving it until another time increases the chances of nothing happening. Achievers use enthusiasm which drives them to immediate action.

'Doing it now' is harder than it sounds. I was in Cairo in 1980 shortly after starting my consulting business. I was doing research for Optrex on a pharmaceutical product, and at the end of the project the last thing I wanted to do was to start writing the report. The research was ready, but the task of unravelling it and putting it into words was daunting.

'I won't start now. I'll wait until I get on the plane,' I thought. 'After all, I deserve a rest and I want to see Cairo, and … and … and …' When the 'ands' got up to about 10, I had to start being honest with myself.

'Are you going to take action now', I asked myself, 'or are you going to let the work pile up and make you depressed? You know you won't do it on the plane. And when you get back, your memory of the details will be dull and your inspiration will be even less than it is today'.

'Hmm', I said back to myself. 'Now that you put it that way, yes, well, I guess I'll do it now.'

I still remember that conversation I had with myself, standing in the middle of my hotel room at the Nile Hilton. I did the report. And you can guess what happened, can't you? It went quicker than I expected, and I had time to see Cairo; have the well-deserved rest, and so on.

If I hadn't done the report, I'd have been miserable because it would have hung over my head. And upon my return, I'd be less happy seeing the new pile of work waiting on my desk, and the report still to do.

Whenever I feel tempted to delay, I think of that day. I still feel sentimental about that conversation in Cairo, and I still like to stay at the Nile Hilton. It gives me good memories of the beginning of my pattern to 'do it now'.

Don't wait for others

In 1965 my husband Tom and I had a chance to take a trip on the SS *France* ocean liner; this was a result of my winning an international sewing competion earlier that year. Little did I know how this trip would shape our lives.

We were thrilled and apprehensive at the same time. It would be our first time travelling on a ship, first class at that, and we wondered what the other people would be like. Would they be millionaires? We knew one thing for sure—they would be earning hundreds and thousands more than we were because we were still impoverished students at university, struggling to make ends meet. What would they have in common with us, we wondered?

The *France* was magnificent. From the deck to the dining room, the service was superb. The decor was fabulous.

The first night of the voyage we entered the elegant dining room. After being introduced at the top of the stairs, we proceeded to our table. It was a large table for eight, and it was there that we met Dr and Mrs Lyle, from Forth Worth, Texas—a couple whose attitude would change our life.

No, the Lyles radiated something special—a warmth and a sincerity of conviction which most people didn't have. We discovered that Dr Lyle was in his 70s and had already contributed much to the medical world in his lifetime. It didn't bother him that the depression in the 1930s had taken away his hard-earned wealth. He just started again.

He told us, 'You can't be afraid to do things you want to do. You can't make excuses and hold yourself back.' The Lyles went on to tell us how they liked doing things for their church and their community. Their contributions were endless.

Dr Lyle worried a lot about young people. If his patients started smoking when they were young, he would get out a pencil and paper and say, 'Look, here's how much money you can save over 40 years if you stop smoking now.' The sum was tremendous. He didn't lecture them on health. He gave them an incentive.

He tried to get people to plan ahead in their lives. If they were worried about money, as most people were, he told them to save before they spent. 'If you wait to start saving after you start spending, you'll find there never is any left'. That's true, isn't it? You have to save first. You have to do it now, no matter how small your income is', he told them.

He even wrote a book called *Practical Living for Today and Tomorrow*. In it he made valuable points he had learned in life which helped people of all ages. He talked about education and marriage and proved his point that the preparation for tomorrow must start today. If we want to achieve the life of our dreams, we have to start now.

Dr Lyle told us about how, some years ago, he made plans to start a hospital. He had invited several doctors to join him in the venture. Many of the doctors were far younger, and had a long future ahead of them. The venture was sound financially, and it would benefit the community tremendously.

Despite the sound prospects, the other doctors hesitated. They faltered. Perhaps fear held them back, but it didn't hold back Dr Lyle. 'If you're going to make major accomplishments in life, you have to take action. You can't wait for those around you.'

Believe nothing is impossible

Some years later, Dr and Mrs Lyle's[1] attitude still rang in our ears. 'You

[1] Judge M. Lyle, MD, *Practical Living for Today and Tomorrow* (Fort Worth, Texas: Lyle-Ballinger Street Medical, no date).

just have to work hard, do what you know is right and believe that anything is possible.' When Tom and I moved from California where we were living to New Jersey, the Lyles suggested that we pass through Colorado and stay at their dude ranch. They wouldn't be there, but their staff would attend to us. Naturally, we jumped at the chance.

The setting of the ranch in the Rocky Mountains was gorgeous. Our children, then aged three, six and seven, thought they were in heaven. We got to know the staff, and they talked to us about Dr Lyle.

'You know, that man thinks anything is possible. He wanted to put a lake in here for fishing and everybody told him it was impossible. He didn't listen. He just kept working until he found someone who thought it was possible.'

Yes, I thought, these are the people who make communities great, who create jobs and put their wealth to work which benefits all. Yes, making the impossible happen does make sense after all. It happens to those who use courage and conviction.

It happened to Walt Disney. He risked his fortune three times in life convincing bankers that animated cartoons and a funpark for adults and kids, called Disneyland, made sense. It happened to Madame Curie when she spent sleepless nights awake in her laboratory with the confiction that a new element could be discovered.

To make the impossible happen, we have to take the first step. As the old adage says, 'A journey of a thousand miles begins with a single step.' We don't know what our capabilities are until we try, nor what they'll develop into as we stretch our threshold of challenge.

I remember when I was 12. My mother suggested I take a sewing class. No, in fact, she insisted I take a sewing class. I was terrified. 'I won't know anyone or anything. How can I possibly go?' I protested. She won the battle and I went.

Little did I know that a few years later my new skill would land me that first trip on the *France*, in competition with 40,000 people from the Singer Company. That trip lead me to Dr Lyle's philosophies. And it lead me to Europe. Without that, I know I wouldn't be living in England now, and perhaps not working in international business.

The first step is most important. The question for all of us is, 'Which steps are necessary to maximize the contribution of ourselves and others?'

Today, in my management consulting, which is primarily concerned with helping companies develop business, I get the opportunity to work with a tremendous variety of company directors. They come first and sit across the conference table, telling us their goals for motivating and training their people for higher performance.

When we start to work together, we learn more about their style of management. I can usually tell from the beginning which ones will be the most successful. They are people who have their end goal clearly in mind. They are people who believe that anything is possible. They are people who have enthusiasm and who take action immediately. They are people who *don't settle for second best* in their own performance— they always stretch themselves to new thresholds.

Undoubtedly, you who are in pursuit of profit already possess many of the qualities. It's people like you to whom Bill Sykes and I address our thoughts. For it is you who will make a difference in this world— in crashing through new thresholds—and encouraging others to do the same.

I remember well a man who attended one of the 'Develop Effective Sales' seminars which Bill and I often run together. Hs name was Dave Phillips and he headed up a publishing group in the north. David had just taken over, and coming from a background of finance, he was eager to absorb as much about sales development as possible.

What made Dave stand out was the enthusiasm and the intensity with which he absorbed the material. Here clearly was a man who intended to use every aspect of the course in managing and motivating his people.

At the end of the seminar, Dave credited Bill and me for running the best course he'd ever attended. Naturally we were delighted, yet the credit should also go to him. *He* had given the course his all and *he* had gained the maximum.

He had formed a mental link between learning and using the material. He had a commitment to using the best techniques to achieve success. On his 'commitment sheet' at the end of the course he had his steps clearly laid out. He had his action plan and he was ready to carry it out immediately. There's no doubt in my mind about Dave's success in business, or about the others like him and like you, who care about motivating yourself and others.

Remember, That a Fundamental Fact About Sales Is:

Success follows those who 'take action now'.

2

Give Them The Facts to Make Their Decision

For years I had been writing articles for a prestigious export magazine. I enjoyed doing it and it was good for my business since it got our name around. After a couple of years people started to say, 'Oh, yes, I've heard of Intrinsic Marketing.' We didn't advertise, so I knew the articles were pulling their weight.

One day I called the magazine to tell them about a new article I was planning to write. Much to my surprise, I was told that the editor-in-chief was no longer there and that a new man had replaced him.

I spoke with the new man briefly. 'I don't take contributions from non-staff writers', he told me. 'But wait', I said, 'I've been contributing to the magazine for years.'

'That may be', he said, 'but the old editor is gone, and I'm running the magazine now. I don't take work from non-staff writers. They don't do the kind of job I require.'

'I'd like to come to see you', I said.

'Come if you like, but you're wasting your time', he said.

His voice was less than encouraging, but I went. I showed him some of the previous articles. I told him that the articles had drawn excellent response from readers. One international banker had even written to say that he was ordering the magazine for his entire department because of my article. He also said that he was keeping it in his public speaking file for reference. 'Hmm', the editor said, 'Well, write something for me and I'll see if I like it.'

I'd never written anything before without having a commitment, and I didn't really want to start now with this man. 'Perhaps we can agree on a subject which we both know will interest the readers', I suggested, 'because I don't write articles without commitment.'

'I never take work from non-staff writers', he said, 'But if you have a good idea, send it to me. I'll look at it.'

I left the building trying to decide what to do. The magazine articles were important to my business. Yet, if I did produce something on speculation as he wanted, I could be wasting my time. After all, I had a business to run and time was valuable.

That night I thought more about the dilemma. If I was going to get anywhere with this new man I'd have to give him something without commitment. After all, he had a business to run too, and he obviously had conviction about the way to do it. So I sat down and wrote an article about entering the export markets. It was concise and hard hitting. Do X, then Y, and don't forget Z.

It took me very little time to write because I had the facts at the tip of my pen. I'd seen British companies attack the US market the right way and the wrong way so many times and vice versa, that I could write the article blindfolded. The next day my office had it typed and sent to the editor.

Two days later I was at London's Heathrow airport, leaving for the States on business. I stopped to call my office before the flight. 'The editor has called and he's anxious to speak to you', they told me. So naturally I called him.

He came to the phone immediately. His whole attitude had changed. 'Oh, Christine', he said, 'the article is fantastic. I hear you're leaving for the States. Can you get me some pictures of yourself there? I'll put your article in our next issue and your picture on the front cover!'

What was there about the article that caused such an abrupt turnaround? I can tell you. The simple truth is that I gave the readers the *facts* they wanted to know about getting into export markets. There was no waffle. It went straight to the point. It sounded like I knew what I was talking about.

It's the same in any business. When people are buying something, they want to be sure that you know the facts about what you're selling. If you have the facts, your credibility goes up because you can answer their questions accurately. If you don't have the facts, a doubt starts to build in their mind. Even if you go back later with the answers, the doubt has had time to simmer and build. They've started to think about alternatives. You may never win them over.

Live and breathe the product—become an authority

It doesn't matter whether we're selling ideas, a service or a product. If we're going to win the buyer over we must have the facts about our product. The article was a service, it was information people could use to improve their sales in other markets. The facts I gave them about this subject were built up over a lifetime of living, working and breathing the business styles abroad.

The editor knew I would have credibility with the readers—who were his buyers—because I had the facts. What credibility do we have with buyers if we don't have the facts about our own product? The buyer is likely to say, 'If this person hasn't got the facts, I'm wasting my time. I might as well go someplace else.' Isn't this true in every industry from domestic appliances to aerospace?

Think back to the last time you went out to buy an electrical appliance. Were the salespeople knowledgeable or did you have to read the literature yourself and compare the features of one model to another?

Maybe your experience was like mine. I spent one Saturday going from one store to another, looking for a dishwasher. 'I want the one which runs the quietest', I told the sales assistant. 'I don't know much about these machines', I was told in the first store. 'Oh, you won't find that out', I was told in the second. 'We only know what's printed on the leaflet'. The third store had no one available to talk to. Their sales people were tied up in another department so long that I decided not to wait.

Finally I stumbled into a last department store. There was a lady in the appliance department who really knew her stuff. 'This one has three cycles, runs 50 minutes maximum. This one has a special filter', and so she continued about each machine. 'What about the quietest?' I asked. 'I want a quiet one for my apartment so it won't disturb me in the next room.' She didn't hesitate with her answer 'Oh, in that case, you want this machine. It had the quietest rating of all machines in the consumer report which was just published last month'. Voila! I was a happy customer. Her product knowledge gave me confidence and I ended my search. She made the sale in five minutes while the other three lost out.

I'm sure I'm not her only satisfied customer. I'm certain that this woman has a high sales performance because she has taken the time and trouble to get to know her product. As I talked to her, I had the feeling she could have continued to give me any fact or figure I needed. She had taken the time and trouble to study the features of each product, to read consumer reports—to live and breathe the product—until she was an authority. I would have hired her on the spot. She was one of the few people who understood the real importance of having all the facts about products in order to sell effectively. And why not? Surely our trade is worth studying. To do less is to deny ourselves of our own potential!

I had a special need—I wanted a quiet machine. The next customer will be just as awkward. They'll have special needs. All customers have special needs. The more facts we have, the more customers we can appeal to.

If this aspect of sales is so self evident, why aren't all salespeople blossoming with facts like this woman? Why haven't they all taken the time and trouble to learn everything they can, until they are authorities?

Perhaps management hasn't made this aspect of sales so self-evident to their people. Perhaps they haven't stopped to realize it themselves.

It doesn't matter what industry you're in. Clients and customers *all* have their own special needs. It's up to you to find their needs and prove we can meet them.

What about service industries? Does the same apply? During one of our seminars to the financial sector, Mark Penny, who is a senior trader for Lloyd's Financial Futures, said he thought it was easier to talk about the benefits of a service than a product.

If you think that the lady with the dishwasher has nothing to do with you, stop and think again. You have to give your buyers the facts to make their decision—you have to prove you can offer the benefits the customer needs—whether you're in banking, stock market trading, accounting, medicine, engineering, consulting or other services—just as those who have a product do. Take Mark Penny's approach. Decide it is easy to relate the benefits to your customer's needs and it will be!

Get the balance right

How many companies do you know that have good products, and pour more and more effort into product development? Yet when it comes to putting effort into improving their sales capability they don't think about giving it the same emphasis.

While I was writing this book, I was interviewed on the Brian Hayes show on LBC Radio in London. Brian asked me whether I thought companies were allocating too much energy to production and not enough to marketing.

'Is there a guideline on the way companies should break down their resources—a percentage which should spent on each?' Brian asked.

What I could tell him is 'That companies which are production oriented often put more energy into production and less into market-ing.' Isn't this natural? We all continue to do more of what we do best.

Yet we have to get the balance right or we run the danger of becoming 'lopsided'.

If you're running a production-oriented company, you may want to sit back and take a look at it. Is the balance right? Could you get more profit, with less effort, by increasing your attention to marketing? Chances are, yes. Most companies can.

Think what results could be achieved with the right emphasis—with everyone trained to know more facts. With knowledge of more product features they would appeal to a wider range of customers. Like the appliance salewoman, their customer base would thrive while the competitors, with less sales competence, would fall to the wayside.

Identify the obstacles

What are some of the obstacles that stand in the way of getting people trained to know more product features—to know the facts inside, outside and upside down? To become high achievers and to help us pursue profit with vigour?

It won't be an easy road ahead. If you hope it will be, you might as well be content with your current profits. It sounds easy to get people to learn about their product, but it isn't. If it was, people like the appliance saleswoman would not be scarce. But she is.

If you're going to pursue profit you have to be a realist and you have to attack obstacles head on. The truth is that salespeople can't always be expected to learn all the product features *without* some form of training—without support from management.

Why? Perhaps because the product is complex and needs explanation. Perhaps it's simple, but the uses of it vary widely. Or perhaps, as we said earlier, they may not have considered how important it is to sell. In that case, you'll have to motivate them. Knowing the features is fundamental to sales—it's the foundation—the base of your pyramid on which everything else will stand. When your people have become an authority like the appliance saleswoman—then your job will be complete. Congratulations—you will have done it!

Now, what system will you use to drill these product features into the minds of everyone? Who will do the drilling? I once worked for a company which wouldn't let the salespeople talk to the service people. But the salespeople were new and the service people were the only ones who knew about the product. The sales manager was told to do the training but he was new too and didn't know any more than the sales people.

Since we were all hired as seasoned salespeople, we knew the fundamentals of selling. We were experts at getting appointments, setting targets and analysing the prospective customer base. We were eager to move. But we didn't know very much about the product. Sound silly? Yes, but it's true, and it happens more often than you think.

Why hire someone and not give them the tools they need to do the job? You're pursuing profit, so you won't make this mistake—you'll give them the tools.

But in devising your effective system for drilling, you'll hit obstacles. What will yours be? Time? Attitude of others? Your own motivation? Money? Lack of ideas? Lack of personnel to organize or carry out the training? You might as well look at your obstacles now, because wanting something is not enough. You'll have to overcome the obstacles.

My good friend Walter Blackburn has a splendid approach to obstacles. Walter is a Dale Carnegie instructor and area manager for part of England. He often runs workshops for people who want to advance their business and personal goals. Walter believes that if we are to achieve our goals we have to look carefully at things that could hold us back. 'If we identify obstacles in our path and plan ways to overcome them, our chances of success are greater', Walter says. Think about that as it relates to training.

One trainer from the United States I know also looks at obstacles. In his workshops on developing power to get things done, he draws the comparison between obstacles and roadblocks. We can either take a detour, or stop there, never reaching our goal.

If Bill and I believed in obstacles, we wouldn't have written this book. It would be easy to let time and other obstacles stand in our way. How could we take the time out to write and still both run our own businesses? How would we communicate our ideas, with the Atlantic between us? And so it goes, obstacles always loom, as they will for you as you bring sales performance to its peak. You'll need to devote time and perhaps money to drilling and you'll need to engender motivation.

Get their support

Let us say you've decided it is necessary to make yourself or your people more of an authority on their product facts. You've overcome the obstacles of time, by deciding to set aside a certain period each day or week until the learning curve is up. Or, let us say you give everyone material to learn in the evening, and test their understanding the next day.

How will you get their support on it? That's a challenging obstacle to overcome. You will probably have to use the technique Dr Lyle used to get people to stop smoking. He gave them an incentive. You can give people incentives by linking their goals to the new training.

I like the illustration Peggy Lindsay teaches in her training courses in Henley (see Figure 1). Peggy shows a wide arrow going diagonally across a page, pointing to the upper right hand corner. This represents the employee's goal. The company goals are represented by another wide arrow going diagonally across the page in the other direction, pointing to the upper left hand corner. The area where the two arrows overlap is the area of common goal. What do you and each of your people have as common goals? When you identify this, you'll have your motivators.

Surely the common goal is to create more sales, especially if your people work on commission. But even then, remember that not all people are motivated by money.

What else will learning the facts do for the individual? Perhaps they'll get more job satisfaction, meet more people, get recognition, adventure— whatever they seek, it's up to us as managers to find out and link their goals to our training. It's not easy. It takes time and effort to get to know people. Peggy's system helps us to visualize the overlap of

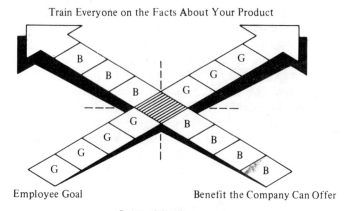

Train Everyone on the Facts About Your Product

Employee Goal   Benefit the Company Can Offer

Point of Overlap =
Motivation for Training

Figure 1   Maximize your motivation

employee and employer goals, and to concentrate our energy at that overlap area.

Make learning easy

There are many reinforcement principles which can help our people get results as they learn. Obviously you'll want to make learning as easy as possible if you want to make your people authorities on your product.

Edward De Bono and others have done interesting studies on the brain to see what techniques make us learn and remember. Since 80% of what we hear is forgotten after two days, your training system will have to include repetition of material, and repetitive testing.

Repeat, repeat, repeat

The British Broadcasting Company, well known worldwide for its excellent productions, ran a German course in conjunction with adult schools which I attended. Anyone could enroll in their local school for the normal course with the instructor. In addition the BBC ran supplemental material for the course four times per week, twice on television and twice on the radio. Those of us learning German could get five repeats each week to reinforce our learning. It was a fabulous system, and all students agreed they learned faster by having the repetitive broadcasts. Therefore, if you want people to remember material, have several ways and varieties of repetition.

Give immediate feedback

Another aspect of learning is immediate feedback. The brain learns best when it receives answers to test questions immediately.

The answers reinforce the learning process. I had a teacher at school I respected above all others. He knew more about learning, motivation and human needs than any I had in all the years of my education.

He was Mr Wisely who taught algebra to 150 of us each year in Glendale, California, and knew the importance of getting immediate reinforcement to the learning process. He devised a selfgrading system for correcting the exam papers immediately after the test. By having the results the same day while the material was fresh in our minds, we learned faster.

Did you ever have an exam at school one week, then get the answers the next week? By the time the answers came, you'd probably forgotten the questions. So give people instant feedback whenever you can.

Give positive, not negative, feedback

What about the learning environment? Your job is to make people learn quickly, not to embarrass them in front of their colleagues. Some people are slower at learning than others. Some people need to ask more questions than others. Bill's background in organizational development has taught him to be sensitive to people's egos. At our seminars he often warns, 'Don't embarrass people publically, even in jest. The person you're embarrassing won't like it and neither will the rest of the group. They'll side with the one being embarrassed, not you.'

I saw Bill's warning exemplified on television shortly after that. The entertainers Little and Large were being interviewed. When the two came on stage, the audience gave them a warm applause. From the smiles on their faces you could tell that the entertainers welcomed the reception. But the interviewer wanted to get the last word. He said, 'Don't let the applause fool you, they're just warming their hands from the snow outside.' A bad joke at the interviewer's expense. It dampened the audience and the mood of the show. Bill was right. The audience sided with those being embarrassed.

The other side of the coin is positive reinforcement. We all learn faster and reach higher performance with positive reinforcement—a kind word of encouragement here and there goes a long way.

Mr Wisely used to write short notes on our homework papers. When we got a difficult problem right, he marked 'GREAT' OR 'EXCEL-LENT' next to the problem. Imagine how good we felt each time we got the paper back.

When we got it wrong he said, 'You were on the right track until this point.' Did we feel deflated? Certainly not—we knew we were on the right track—Mr Wisely said so, he encouraged us. He didn't say 'You went wrong here.' There's a big difference, one is positive, one is negative.

Are we any different when we're 40 than when we're 14? No, we all need positive encouragement. I worked hard in Mr Wisely's class and did better than in any other class. Don't we want that dedication and high performance from our people when we pursue profit?

Why not give a little encouragement like Mr Wisely did? It doesn't take long and it gets big results.

I remember the woman who taught me to sew. She was a master of motivation for achieving perfection. When we did something wrong, she didn't ridicule us. She simply said, 'This has got to go.' When we did it right she examined it carefully and praised us for doing the job well. Somehow we all ended up doing our best for Dorothy Kearns. I'm sure she's still in California helping others to do their best. Is there any doubt in your mind about why her technique works? She didn't place judgement on the work or the person. She just stated 'This has to go.' This helped people not to feel discouraged about themselves in a learning environment. Think about it. Can you change your wording to remove negativity and judgement? If you do, you'll be amazed at the results, both in terms of personal relationships and in motivating others.

Charles Schwab, who back in the 1920s was paid over a million dollars a year for this ability to manage people, said, 'People work better and give greater effort under a spirit of approval than they ever do under a spirit of criticism!'

Isn't this good advice for you and me in motivating our people? Most people learn and thrive in a supportive environment. When managers learn to increase their supportiveness, giving each person specific positive feedback, they get an overwhelming increase in results. The same is true of parents with children, and vice versa—after all, aren't we all managers when it comes to human relationships?

Get competitive

What else motivates people to learn? Most sales people like competitiveness. A little competition could spark up your training. That algebra teacher who knew so well how to motivate, had another effective gimmick. He used to reassign seats after each exam according to the score each person achieved. The first row on the left had the highest achievers. Imagine it. It wasn't just an 'Honour Roll' posted on a notice board in some obscure corner. No, there was a physical presence of the high achievers there for all to see.

As the 'winners' sat in the seats of that first row, do you think they absorbed that feeling of success? Do you think they wanted to let it go? No, they were determinated to keep it and they tried harder each week. So did the others—they tried to overtake one another, and before long the standard of the whole group went up. They were untouchable. No one in the school could match the standards of Mr Wisely's people.

Do we want our people to be unbeatable? Let's give them competition and recognition.

Do you know who in your group knows more product features than anyone else? Find out. Acknowledge them. Give the others a standard to beat.

Sound gimmicky, childish? Of course it does, but it works because there's a little bit of kid in all of us. And a little competitiveness. Why not work *with* human nature, not *against* it. It makes sense.

The next time someone reproaches you for using gimmicky methods of competition, remind them about human nature—and let them see the results before they condemn. You'll have the winning team, not them.

Set a high standard

What about this concept of training people to learn more facts about the product? We know it will improve their performance, but isn't it awkward to suddenly bring in a new training philosophy?

Do we really have the right to impose rigid learning practices on our people? The answer is yes, emphatically yes. They love it—or learn to.

I hear that Arthur Andersen, the international accounting and consulting firm, flies its consulting trainees from wherever they work worldwide to Chicago for three weeks of solid hard indoctrination. They train and test seven days a week, from morning till night. The evening and weekend sessions are 'optional' but anybody missing them will probably not pass the rigid exams along the way.

This is good preparation for the dedication to the job which the consultants give to Arthur Andersen after the training. I know several people who work for Arthur Andersen now, and I can tell you it would be hard to find better trained, more dedicated employees than these. They don't quit until the job is done, no matter how late or how hard they work. And their customers appreciate it.

Wouldn't we all like to instill this dedication in our people? Why not start with a good solid training system and set a high standard for everyone to live up to?

I remember from my Dale Carnegie training, one of the most useful courses I've ever attended, that we learned to give people a reputation to live up to. If we set a high standard, people do rise to the occasion. Best of all, they feel good about themselves.

We can look to other success stories—IBM, Proctor and Gamble—

they all devote substantial time to training. So do small companies which are successful. And employees expect to burn a little midnight oil in doing their job and in learning, if the pressure from management says it's necessary.

It's as true in Britain as it is in America. Arthur Anderson proves it works around the world.

If we set a high standard for our people by expecting them to become authorities on the product, it will set the scene for them to become high achievers in other facets of sales.

Bill Sykes tells the story of Michael Beer who once worked for Parker Pen. Once Michael had the opportunity to drive through his town with Mr Parker who pointed out every jewellery and stationery store asking if that store stocked their pens. But Mr Parker didn't stop there. He expected Michael to know every aspect of their business—which inks were purchased, what typewriters, what percentage of the business they had, did they do their own service and so on.

Mr Parker didn't settle for second best. He expected his people to know everything, not just product features, but anything and everything about the customer. If we're in pursuit of profit, shouldn't we expect the same?

Be inventive

Perhaps you're in need of training ideas in order to make your people authorities on your product or service. If so, why not be inventive? In one company I worked with when I was new, I went out to interview satisfied customers about how they used our product. I made this part of my training exercise. Then I wrote the results of the interviews up as case studies. Then, combined with photographs, the case studies were used as press releases and promotions.

While doing the interview, I discovered new facts about the products and got quotes from the customers which we used later in selling. We understood the customers better and our enthusiasm grew.

Was it a long process? No. The whole exercise of setting up the interview, carrying it out and writing it up, took less than a day of time for each case study.

And here's the best part. New business resulted from two out of the six companies interviewed. The customers had their interest heightened during the interview and placed new orders with the company. That was an unexpected fringe benefit. It proves what can be done when we use imagination in developing methods which train and motivate our people.

What imaginative learning exercise would work in your business? Don't discount any new idea until you've given it a chance. Einstein said, 'Imagination is more important than intelligence.' Let's not be so intellectual and traditional that we fail to be imaginative. Let's upgrade our sales skills through *every* source possible.

Remember, That a Fundamental Fact About Sales Is:

Make sure your salespeople become authorities so that they can give customers the facts.

3

Bring Your Benefits into the Open

'Eat your vegetables, they're full of vitamins,' said little Johnny's parents to Johnny. But little Johnny didn't know what vitamins were. He didn't see what good they would be to him. Neither did the buyer of the Xerox 295 Facsimile when the salesman told him, 'It uses the latest high-speed Group 3 digital transmission technology.'

'Oh?,' said the buyer. He was as confused as little Johnny. He knew about as much about high speed digital technology as Johnny knew about vitamins—and cared less. What would that do for him? He only wanted to send copies of contracts from his office in London to his colleages in Australia.

Remember that people buy only the benefits, not the features

Then the salesman went on to say, 'This means you can send and receive copies at the speed of a phone call—in fact, in 28 seconds!'

'Whew, now we're getting somewhere,' thought the buyer. 'I'll take one.'

The salesman finally told him the benefit he would receive from digital technology. The benefit met his needs, so he bought. People don't buy the features of our products and services, they buy the benefits.

Not long ago a client of ours from Britain, dealing with laboratory equipment, went to the United States to market his product. He had a superb product with a lot of technical features. What did he do when he got in front of the buyer? He did what most people do. He fell into the trap of telling the buyer all the features, but didn't explain the benefits.

Luckily Bill was there with him and brought him to a halt. 'Wait a minute, Peter; could you back up over that brown etched line on the thermometer. Why is that important?' asked Bill.

'Oh, well, most of our competitors have painted lines. Those are less precise than ours. With our etched line you get a more accurate reading.'

The buyer's eyes lit up. 'A more accurate reading—oh, that's very interesting,' said the buyer. Previously, while our client had talked about the brown etched line, he had been nodding in agreement. But obviously hadn't recognized the benefit. Why should he? After all, he dealt with hundreds of suppliers. He had a catalogue of 30,000 different pieces of equipment. He couldn't be expected to know the benefits of them all.

Why should any buyer, for that matter, recognize the benefits if we don't tell them what they are? People are no different than little Johnny, or the Xerox buyer. They don't know unless we tell them. And they won't buy unless they recognize the benefit. Remember this the next time you want to convince *anyone* of *anything*!

Identify a benefit for every feature of your product

In our sales development seminar, Bill and I throw the attendees straight into an exercise on benefits. They're asked to bring information about one particular product or service so that it can act as the base of their activity throughout the course. Their first task is to circulate around the room and tell each of the other attendees the benefits of their own product. They have 60 seconds to tell each person, then rotate to the next.

Can you guess what happens? They soon start falling into the trap into which our client Peter and most people fall. They tell the features, not the benefits. In fact, they often have difficulty at first, trying to decide what the benefits are for each product. But we don't despair.

With thought and practice, people become proficient at identifying the benefits of the product. Then they can start applying it to increase sales. The results can be dramatic. From this exercise alone we have people who come to the seminars around the world, write to tell us later that they got a 30% higher increase in sales just from stressing the benefits. Think about how you can put a push on benefits in your own business.

Talk, write and think benefits

Benefits should be used in *all* of the following areas:

- Sales presentations
- Literature
- Advertising
- Contracts and proposals
- Letters
- Getting appointments
- In management meeting to make our point
- In public speaking to make our point
- In personal life to make our point

Some people are naturals when it comes to talking about benefits. One client was telling me not long ago about the machinery his company had developed for making data processing labels. 'This machine cuts raw material costs by 25%,' he said. 'Any company overseas should be delighted to work with us on a licensing basis – think of the money we can save them!'

No wonder Laurence Bloom has been able to lead his company, Stampiton near Manchester, to a prominent position. He knows people want to hear benefits and he goes straight to them. Did you hear Laurence talk about features? Did he say, 'Our machine has the technology to coat the release paper in-line while it's producing the labels?' No, he skipped the feature altogether.

He went straight to the benefit. If we want to talk about the features, we can do that later. First let's talk about the benefit. Everyone understands that. Let's capture their interest with the benefit and move on to features later.

But Laurence is an expert. He started his own company ten years ago and now he's a director of other companies as well. He's learned to 'talk benefits'. He's learned to 'write benefits'. He's probably learned to 'think benefits'. And he's had results. But can our people talk, write and think benefits? Perhaps they don't have Laurence's know-how. Most people don't. But with practice *everyone* can improve.

If we can get benefits engrained in the minds of everyone, think of the results that can be achieved. Let's look closer to gain a better understanding for our own company.

What holds people back from either recognizing or discussing the benefits? Obviously they have to know what they are before they can use them in selling. In looking closely at this problem, Bill and I see that there are three things standing in the way:

Don't think that benefits are obvious

Firstly, they are often so close to a product that they think the benefit is obvious to the buyer. So they don't bring it out into the open.

Of course, it's never as obvious to the buyer as it is to those of us who work with the product day in and day out. Did Laurence think the 'technology to coat the release paper in-line' would be obvious to us? No. But a technician who works closely with the machinery might think it was obvious because he's so close to it.

If we're in pursuit of profit, we must get our people to ignore what seems obvious to them. They must talk benefits first. Let features follow.

What about the microprocessor salesman who goes into the buyer and says, 'This is fully upwardly compatible with our earlier 16-bit machine and completes the progression of the 8-, 16-, and now 32-bit members of a single family of microprocessors.' He's close to his product too. By the time he had finished, his buyer was asleep.

For him that feature 'fully upwardly compatible', may be so obvious to him that he doesn't explain the benefit. But the buyer needs to hear the benefit, 'This means you can expand the capability of your hardware easily.' We *must* state the benefit.

Don't confuse the benefit with the feature

The second thing holding people back from recognizing their own benefits is that they get confused about the difference between features and benefits. For the Xerox 295 salesman, it's easy to see that the 'latest high speed digital transmission technology' is the feature. What's the benefit? 'You get copies fast.'

But some people would be tempted to say, 'The machine works fast.' They would falsely think of that as the benefit. But it's not. 'The machine works fast' still talks about the machine just like 'high speed technology' talks about the machine. Whereas, 'you get fast copies', talks about what the customer gets.

When we tell what the customer gets, we're talking benefits.

One seminar attendee we had was enthusiastic about benefits and wanted to present his own benefits to our group. We gave him two minutes to come up to the flip chart and tell us. For the first minute and a half he talked about the wiring configuration inside his telecommunications product. I stopped him and said, 'Bob, when do we get to hear what the customer gets? You only have 30 seconds left'. He said, 'I can't tell you the benefits until you understand how it works!' He had missed the point.

We then asked him more about the customer's needs until he was able to state the benefits they receive in a simple way, forgetting the complex wiring. 'Oh', he said in astonishment, 'Now I think I know why no one at work understands me when I give demonstrations. Now I know I have to talk about what the product does, not how it works! Thanks.'

He suddenly realized the great advantage he would have in communication by talking about the benefits the user receives *first*. This puts everyone in the picture. Then, when the scene is set, he can talk about features.

Don't be afraid of being personal

The third thing holding people back from discussing benefits is their fear of being too personal or too direct. Of all the countries we work in, this is more true in England than in others. The English are more reluctant to touch on personal issues.

And, since benefits do relate to people, this is a legitimate concern. But there are ways to overcome it. We don't need to hit the buyer over the head with the benefit. We don't need to say, 'Since you're so overweight, this slimming class will be good for you.' What we can do is to use a third party reference. We can say 'Mr Jones came to the slimming class at the beginning of last month, and already he has made great progress. He's playing tennis now which he's always wanted to do. Everyone who comes regularly to the class benefits.' This eliminates being too personal and whets the buyer's appetite for the benefits.

This reference to another person is very effective. Remember it regardless of what you're selling. Use it and your sales will skyrocket.

Use benefits in all aspect of life

Remember the third party reference in personal life too. The next time you want to convince your daughter or son or wife or husband or anyone in your life to do something, think of the benefit and then tell them about it. Tell the story as it benefits someone else. It will whet their appetite and motivate action.

Talk about benefits in your literature, in your advertising and in the letters you write every day. Talk about benefits at management meetings, and the next time you speak to a group. It will work wonders. Use it to benefit your community.

What if you want your Rotary group to accept 'Guide Dogs for the Blind' for their charity, as Mic Bryant, a friend of mine in England, did? Perhaps you can tell them a moving story about how someone you know benefited from having a guide dog.

Let them know the feeling of community pride they themselves will gain from supporting this cause. Capture their hearts and minds. Perhaps you'll be as successful as Mic was. His group went on to present the results of their charity to the Guide Dogs for the Blind Association at the House of Commons in London. Think what more we can accomplish for society when we help others to focus on benefits.

Do you ever need to influence the opinions of an audience? The Chairman of Sony Corporation of Japan knows how to use benefits to convince. I saw him hold an audience of 4,500 people spellbound at the Albert Hall in 1982, at the Institute of Directors Convention, when he discussed the future of robotics. Would robots endanger the workforce? Mr Akio Morita likened the advent of robotics to the advance of computers.

He reminded us of the benefits of the computer industry and the jobs created. He focused our mind on the benefits of job creation when new technology emerges. As he spoke in English while referring to his notes in Japanese, he awed us with his ability to sway opinion. He stressed benefits in order to make his point—benefits which everyone could relate to.

No wonder this man has brought his company into a leading world position. If he can use benefits to sway a group of over 4,000 in a language second to his own, think what we can do in our own companies and our own community. Let's start at home like Mic Bryant did to help the community. Let's improve our business by stressing benefits now and watch the results we get.

Remember, a Fundamental Fact of Sales Is:

Talk Benefits first, second and third. Talk Features later.

Review of Part One

Fundamental Facts You Should Know about Sales

Chapter 1 Maximize the Contribution of Ourselves and Others

1. Conquer Challenges at Each Threshold
2. Advance Your Goals and Self Image
3. Influence Others to Develop Patterns of Highest Achievement
4. Acknowledge Strengths and Weaknesses
5. Do it Now
6. Don't Wait for Others
7. Believe Nothing is Impossible

Chapter 2 Give Them the Facts to Make Their Decision

1. Live and Breathe the Product—Become an Authority
2. Get the Balance Right
3. Identify the Obstacles
4. Get Their Support
5. Make Learning Easy
   Repeat, repeat, repeat
   Give Immediate Feedback
   Give Positive, Not Negative Feedback
   Get Competitive
6. Set a High Standard
7. Be Inventive

Chapter 3   Bring Your Benefits into the Open

1. Remember that People Buy Only the Benefits, Not the Features
2. Identify a Benefit for Every Feature of Your Products
3. Talk, Write and Think Benefits
4. Eliminate the Benefit Roadblocks
      Don't Think that the Benefit is Obvious
      Don't Confuse the Benefit with the Feature
      Don't be Afraid of Being Personal
5. Use Benefits in All Aspects of Life

Part One Action Sheet

Ideas for Development:

- Make sales people authorities

- Stress benefits first, features later

-

-

-

-

-

-

Of the above ideas, which one is likely to yield the best results?

What percentage of sales (or performance) increase could realistically be expected?

How long would it take:
  to develop the idea?
  to get results?

Who would have to be involved?

What date should we start?

What is the first step I should take?

PART TWO
The Perfect Way To Motivate

4

Remember This and You Will Succeed

The way we learn and the way we behave is inseparable from motivation. Anyone who has studied psychology remembers the lesson of Pavlov and his contemporaries. Given an animal a training area, shock it when it goes off course, reward it when it reaches the end goal. Very soon it goes directly to the end goal without deviating. Is this not what we want from our employees? For that matter is it not what we want from everyone—our worldwide friends and foes, our spouses, our children?

Human beings are more complex, yet Pavlov's theories have something to teach us. If we want to motivate people to do things our way, we have to remember that we're only really running a learning area—a very scientific learning area where every step along the path is in the right or wrong direction.

Did Pavlov and his fellow scientists wait until the animal stumbled onto the end goal to give his reward? Of course not. That would take too long. It would be too chancy. Instead they gave the animal small rewards along the way, to guide it, encourage it, to give it specific direction. This accelerated reaching the end goal. It left nothing to chance.

Are we leaving motivation to chance? Do we give lip service to motivation, but let the employees go in all directions unnoticed? Do we sometimes reward them and sometimes not, leading to confusion, then blame them for being unpredictable? Do we even know what the end goal is, or do we wait until people go in the wrong direction and then lambast them for not finding their own way to the undetermined goal?

It sounds ridiculously simple and obvious when we relate it to Pavlov and the animal. But in reality many of us are trying to motivate people in our business and personal life without direction.

Do people tell their spouses what they really want from them to help them make our lives together a success? Or do they let them guess at it for 20 years and then, when they're wrong, they divorce them? Do we talk with our colleagues and employees to find out what their goals in life are, then plan a path that meets both the company's and the employee's objectives? If so, then everyone profits.

Experts in motivational psychology say that a person's happiness is directly proportional to the speed at which they are moving towards their goal. Can we not then help them find goals which also meet our objectives, or in business, the company's objectives? Frame of mind is all important. If we can keep people moving toward goals, we keep the level of satisfaction up. We keep a positive cycle going.

So we see from scientists like Pavlov that the learning process is scientific. When we bring it down to basics, it's a two-part process. When the subject of the training goes off the track, it gets punishment, specific negative feedback. When it's on track, it gets reward, specific positive feedback. Naturally, the trainer knows the end goal.

The pessimist would argue that people are more complex than animals and that such a simple theory will not work in motivating people. The optimist would argue that the animal is more difficult to motivate than the human—after all, the human can communicate.

With the human we can explain and agree on the path to be taken. We can even ask what specific rewards and reinforcements the human likes along the way. Not only can we ask, we should ask, for anyone going along a path which is against their will is bound to resent it.

So the optimist would see the job as easier than Pavlov's. The optimist would define the maze, agree the terms and get started on the specific reward system. The optimist would see the job as easy. The optimist would succeed.

The pessimist would dwell on the complexity of human nature. The pessimist would say that it's not possible to motivate people by agreeing on goals which benefit both parties and would see reward systems as simplistic.

The pessimist would talk himself out of putting the animal in the maze, and then blame the beast for being undisciplined—for needing motivation in the first place.

He would reason, 'After all, shouldn't everyone hired for a job know where they're going and how to get there. Isn't that their job?' The pessimist would never get a start and therefore not succeed.

So let's go with the optimists' theory where results are possible. At the same time, let's rectify some of the concerns for the pessimist by refining the system.

Let's look at punishment and reward. Do the scientists use 50 megavolts of electricity which knocks the beast dead when it goes off track? No, of course not. They use a subliminal shock which is so faint that the animal doesn't consciously recognize it. The shock is only enough to force its attention in another direction. We also don't want to kill the subject's enthusiasm, rather just turn the direction.

Pavlov's success is in the reward system. The reward gives positive feedback that the subject is on the right course. It makes conscious impression on the subject. It builds a reinforcement in the brain's mental links which makes a repeat performance become more automatic. Each reward reinforces that link so that the performance becomes more and more automatic.

Let's look at the reward more closely. With all scientific formulas, the ingredients must be specifically right for each purpose we want to achieve. Would we use bird food to reward a dog, or horse meat to reward fish? Doubtful. Common sense tells us otherwise.

Why then do we think we can reward one person with something we like, or someone else likes, or the masses like? Shouldn't we reward with reinforcement which is specifically right for that individual's needs and goals?

We find out what's right in the beginning when we define the path with the individual. But even then we'll not have success unless we're specific with our reward.

Let's imagine we have a path with five points along it leading to the end results. When our subject gets to the right point we want to tell them they've arrived. We don't want to say 'You're about there.' Otherwise, they'll keep looking for the exact point.

Yet in management we find people who think vague acknowledgement is reinforcement. They haven't learned that exact, specific feedback is necessary to get the subject to the end goal in the shortest possible time.

They think a smile, a nod or even the lack of punishment is enough to keep people on course!

Let's be realistic. Would the subject in Pavlov's work have learned without having food as a specific reward at the end? Would it have understood a smile or a nod or the lack of punishment to be the signal that it had arrived? Or would there be uncertainty? Would it wonder if it should proceed to the next step or try to perfect its current position?

The point is that to motivate people effectively we must use specific positive feedback. We must tell them exactly what they did which was correct. 'Nice job, John,' may be a good start, but it's not specific.

If you want to give reinforcement which gets results you'll include exactly what was done and what affect it had. 'John, I appreciate the fact that you worked all weekend to meet the deadline. That section of the proposal on pricing was a masterpiece. The numbers were laid out in a format which was concise and easy to read. Thanks, John; if we win the bid, it's due to your excellent contribution.'

Here's an amazing fact recently discovered from a survey in the United States. In the first grade, 60% of the children think they 'can do it'. In other words 60% have confidence they can accomplish any new task set out. By the sixth grade, guess how many think they 'can do it'. Only 10%.

With adults, the job is more difficult. We have to provide a supportive environment for them to excel. We have to give positive feedback.

This technique of specific feedback can be used in any situation in which you want to give people the credit they deserve. In a sales seminar Bill and I might say to each other, 'I really liked the way you involved the participants in the second session by relating the material to their industries and to them personally. I noticed that those particular people took a stronger leadership role later on.' It takes *more* thought than a casual comment, but with motivation you're looking for *more* than a casual commitment.

It's important to be specific. Financial people relate well to the importance of specifics. They wouldn't dream of working with figures 'vaguely in the range of such and such', so why should we work with vague feedback. It simply doesn't tell anybody anything.

The use of specific positive feedback, whether in business, social or personal life, has lasting results. It's the perfect way to motivate. It's easy to use and easy to remember if we keep an analogy such as Pavlov in mind. We need only to agree the end goal, then reinforce the steps along the way.

Remember, The Perfect Way To Motivate Is To:

Agree on Goals and Be Specific In Your Feedback

5

Leadership is for Everyone

Do we need high performance? The Japanese think so. I remember well a conversation I had with a business acquaintance in Tokyo in late 1985. We had a very interesting discussion about the business and cultural differences between the English, the Americans, the Germans and the Japanese.

Then he told me that the GNP in Japan was catching up to America. He was sure it would pass America before 1995—less than a 10-year period.

'You know, Christine,' he said 'we have a commitment here that westerners don't understand. People take their careers and their responsibilities seriously here. Perhaps you could say too seriously.

'I'll tell you the truth. If a manager of a major company is given a very important job—let's say to develop a new machine cheaper and better than the rival competitor—then the success in this job means a major promotion.

'Failure means demotion to a nondescript position, never to resurface again. I guarantee that person will do everything in their power to succeed on time, within budget. And if they fail? They may well commit suicide—that is the seriousness of commitment!'

As I sat in the palatial surroundings of the hotel in Tokyo I thought about commitment. Yes, my friend was right, that is a commitment westerners don't understand. But, if we were in that environment long enough, or were born into it, we would understand it. We would live by it.

Tell them what's expected

The same is true of leaders. If you set the right environment for people, they develop leadership. If you set a lax environment, they develop laxness.

If we want our people to learn to have commitment, we have to:

- Tell them what they are expected to accomplish in their job and
- Set the standard they are expected to reach

Bill remembers well the practices of his first boss, Piers Flashman at Horlicks Pharmaceutical company. Piers was one of the early influences on Bill because his management style was so effective.

Piers always took the time with his employees in delegating responsibility. He didn't assume that they knew what the end goal was. He took time to make sure the job objective was clearly laid out.

Bill remembers when they were faced with a massive job of setting up a new pharmaceutical research laboratory. This required purchasing equipment, moving people and so on. Piers would explain, 'Now I'm taking responsibility for the building contract, and I want you to be responsible for sales administration, and so on.'

Regardless of the pressure he was under, he would stop at the end of the day to make sure everyone understood their responsibilities.

Bill and his colleagues who were just out of college thrived under this leadership. People must know where they're going in order to have the commitment to get there.

Bill, in his organizational development work, sees examples often within companies of managers presuming employees know how to handle a task and know what end result is expected. They don't. Sometimes they don't see the obvious unless we show them.

What is the most obvious—but overlooked—ability we must develop in people if they are to assume responsibility and leadership?

It's the ability, not just to take action, but to get the end goal accomplished. That's the most important standard we can set for them. It's a standard that can last a lifetime and make or break their ability for leadership.

If you ask an employee, 'Call the bank and get information about opening an account,' you don't mean you want some information. You mean you want all the information necessary to open the account. Most employees who eventually fail in leadership think their job is finished when they get whatever information the bank gives them.

They don't stop to question whether the information meets the end goal. They don't ask. 'Do I now have the complete information necessary to open the account?'

No, many think their job is done because they were told to call the bank and they did. They tried to get information. They got information. But they didn't take it to the 'logical' conclusion. That gap, that bridge between the task and the end results, is the leadership gap.

Teach the difference between trying and doing

Surely if we have everyone reaching the end result and not just working on the task, our companies will benefit. How can people be taught to bridge that gap?

First we have to make people aware of the leadership gap—the difference between 'just trying' and 'accomplishing'.

A psychologist I know uses a very powerful technique to demonstrate this difference.

She starts by throwing a pencil on the floor. Then she says, 'Try to pick up that pencil.' As people bend over and almost touch it, she says, 'Wait, I said try to pick it up, not pick it up.'

Do you see the meaning of try? We either do it or we don't. 'Trying' and 'accomplishing' are two different things.

Let's look at our employee who was calling the bank. Let's say you want to invest some company money for a short period of time and you need to know the interest rate and the withdrawal details. There is an overnight call account and a two-day notice account. You want details on both US dollars and Japanese yen.

Your employee calls the bank. The manager is in a meeting and the foreign clerk's line is busy.

A second call reveals that the bank manager knows some answers, but not all of them, and will have his foreign clerk get all the details.

A third call reveals that the foreign clerk knows the interest rate but is unclear about the withdrawal terms.

This goes on and on. If your employee thinks their job is to actually *get* all the information, *not just try* to get it, they will *probe* until they get the answers they need. That's the value of a leader—one who can be counted on to 'accomplish'—not just try.

Tackle even small tasks relentlessly

If a person can be trained to tackle the above task relentlessly, they will learn to handle bigger management problems the same way. 'From little acorns, big oaks grow.' Simple, effective and true.

Just as Bill's first boss knew, people have to understand the expected end result if they are to develop leadership.

By holding people responsible for small complete tasks, we are nurturing leadership for the future. We're nurturing commitment to high standards which achieve results.

How do we foster this leadership, this commitment to high standards which get results? As managers, we have to start with ourselves. We have to stand for high performance.

We have to stand for performance that gets results.

John Cougar Mellencamp had a hit song that swept the charts. It said, 'You've got to stand for somethin', or you're going to fall for anything.'

We have to be known for a motto which says 'trying' isn't enough. When people know you stand for something they recognize you as leaders. They follow in your footsteps.

Then we help people bridge the leadership gap.

One of my past employees who I most admire is Anne-Joelle Galley. What first struck me about Anne-Joelle is that she was never afraid to ask questions or contribute her opinions, and they are always valued opinions. When given a task, she always probed to get all the details. She always made sure she knew the expected end results.

This dynamic young woman has spent most of her life divided between Switzerland and Mexico. When I asked her for the secret of her success she told me, 'I always feel it's better to stand up and make a decision and have it be wrong, than to not make a decision at all.' That's the way she felt people could progress and not stagnate. If everyone took this attitude our companies would prosper from a wealth of new ideas and improvements. Yet fear often stands in their way.

It's up to people to overcome their fear, as Anne-Joelle did, realizing it would help her progress. It's also up to managers to create a safe environment for this to happen.

When we offered Anne-Joelle a job with us in London she said she could have chosen the easy way, that would be to stay in her home town in Switzerland where there were no uncertainties. Instead she chose to come to England, a country where she knew no one. She would face the uncertainty of opening new horizons.

It's the same in management. If we take on a new job, like fostering leadership, we face uncertainties. We open up new horizons. We grow. Our leadership ability grows. We're soon faced with more situations which come to us because we're able to stand for something. People rely on our leadership ability. It's then that we get results second to none.

Remember, The Perfect Way To Motivate Is To:
Stand For 'Trying isn't Enough'

Review of Part Two

The Perfect Way to Motivate

Chapter 4   Remember This and You Will Succeed

1. Agree on Goals
2. Be Specific in Your Feedback

Chapter 5   Leadership is for Everyone

1. Sell Them What's Expected
2. Teach the Difference Between Trying and Doing
3. Tackle Even Small Tasks Relentlessly

Part II Action Sheet

Ideas for Development:

- Agree on goals and be specific in giving feedback
- Recognize how others are motivated and develop a common ground for trust
- Insist on results, even on the smallest task, Stand for 'trying isn't enough'
-
-
-
-
-

Of the above ideas, which one is likely to yield the best results?

What percentage of sales (or performance) increase could realistically be expected?

How long would it take:
   to develop the idea?
   to get results?

Who would have to be involved?

What date should we start?

What is the first step I should take?

PART THREE
Basic Techniques
To Make Buying Easy

6

Help the Customers to Recognize Their Needs

Let's imagine that a consumer buys a home and has to start furnishing it. They have to buy things for every room. They're under pressure and they're in a new town. They don't know quite what to buy or where to find everything. But it must be finished in two weeks and ready to live in.

In most businesses, including highly technical businesses, our customers are similar to the customers above. They need to accomplish something under time pressure because of deadlines of the demands of the job. They don't know quite what's available to meet their requirements, but they must solve their problem soon.

Get the customer to verbalize needs

Perhaps the consumer hasn't had time to examine every aspect of their needs.

They only know they need the house furnished. They may not, under time pressure, decide on the exact size and shape of the furniture until they see what's available. The smart salesperson will help them analyse their needs. They will then suggest ways they can help—ways their furniture will fit the consumer's needs.

The salesperson might ask:

'Do you want a casual or a formal atmosphere?'

'Are your rooms large or small?'

'Do you need it now, or can you wait for delivery?'

The smart salespeople will ask questions and get the customers to verbalize their needs.

There must be something in our brains that acts like a rubber stamp. When prospective customers verbalize a need, it becomes indelibly stamped on their brain. It's true in all businesses. If customers don't state their needs, often they aren't quite clear about what their needs are. By asking questions we help them to put their need into focus.

Often, because prospects don't know everything that's on the market, they express their needs broadly rather than specifically.

We often have prospective clients coming into our office for an initial consultation who tell us that they want to 'increase sales'. That's good as a broad base, but we need to use the questioning process to get them to identify specific needs. We might ask which markets they now deal in. Or which they would like to enter or do better in.

Every business has its own needs and we can get customers to recognize those needs by asking the right questions.

Questioning is essential. Prospects who are told exactly what a product does, its benefits and why they should buy it are *not* yet being convinced. However, when they are asked questions about their needs, their answers reinforce their reason for buying. They become involved in the buying process.

Probe for needs with questions

Most prospects are happy to be asked questions about their needs. In fact they are pleased that someone cares enough about their problems to ask and to listen. It helps to build an atmosphere in which the prospects feel they are buying rather than being sold to. No one in sales should be afraid to ask questions because most people appreciate it.

To put yourself in the frame of mind to ask questions effectively, think of yourself as a buying facilitator, not a seller. Or think of yourself as a consultant diagnosing the problem and proposing alternatives. Your goal is to have the prospects feel you're on their side, helping them to get the outcome which suits them best.

Recognize the need or lose the sale

Occasionally people resist the questioning process. But they can be persuaded to see the value of the questioning line in two ways.

- by explaining your reasons for questions
- by asking their permission.

We find it useful, after initial ice breaking, to start the meeting by saying something like this: 'Mr Smith, since there's not enough time today for you to tell us everything about your company, nor us to tell you everything about ours, perhaps we could start by giving you an overview of our service. Then you'll be in a better position to tell us your needs as they relate to these. By the end of the meeting we should be able to see whether there is an area of mutual interest. If there is, then we can tell you about our service in detail. Would that be OK?'

If we tried to tell them all our services from beginning to end, or listened to their company history without guiding them to their needs through the questioning process, their needs would never be clarified. They would leave in despair. The questioning process keeps the discussion on track because every question is designed to bring both sides closer to understanding the needs and agreeing on solutions.

Usually most people go along with this. It makes sense. However, some people continue to resist the questioning process. To overcome this you can re-explain the necessity to confine your discussion to their needs. 'I know you want to leave here today with a clear understanding of how our service relates to your company rather than talk in generalities.'

We showed one prospective client a list of services early in our meeting and he revealed that he wasn't interested in export but preferred to license his technology. It would have been a shame for us to explain our export assistance service rather than licensing if we hadn't known about his needs.

You may fear that you run the chance of losing the prospect by continuing to seek information about their need. But remember that if you don't get your key features and benefits effectively over to the prospects as it relates to their needs, you'll lose the sale anyway. So make a commitment to help customers recognize their needs. The way is simple. Ask.

Remember, to Make Buying Easy:

**Become proficient at asking questions.
When prospects answer they are identifying and
reinforcing their buying motive.**

7

Don't Sell—Let Them Buy

Several years ago one of our management trainees did a comparative study on word processors. We reviewed the literature and invited the best company to do a demonstration for us. I had approved the expenditure and the sale was theirs, pending the success of the demonstration.

The day came, and two people arrived to do the demonstration. They didn't ask us what we hoped to use the machine for. They just launched into their standard demonstration. We were terribly busy that day and only wanted to see one feature—the one which would merge letters with addresses. We thought the machine could handle this based on its literature and previous discussions with the company.

We asked about the address merging feature but neither of them could demonstrate this facility nor did they act the least bit interested in our questions. They continued with the standard demonstration.

Identify the benefits which are most important to each customer

Why did neither of them seem to care about our needs? Why didn't they reassure us that the machine had that capability, or offer to find out how it worked and come back? Were they afraid to admit they didn't know? Did they really think they could ignore our needs and sell the machine by demonstrating features which didn't relate to our needs? Or, did they perhaps not understand the importance of our question to the selling process? Whatever it was, they lost the sale.

When leaving, the two salespeople made no apology or attempt to address our need. They asked some standard closing questions which didn't relate to us.

Little did they know that 25 minutes earlier when they walked in the door the sale was practically in their hand!

Nothing stood in the way except their ability to hear our need and respond to it. Is it possible that they hadn't heard our questions about merging letters with addresses? Perhaps their mind was so intent on going through a standard list of features, that they didn't recognize the importance of our questions.

Perhaps they felt it was their duty to explain all the standard features even though we were only interested in one—the one they couldn't explain.

The next day we saw a different machine which suited us and we bought that. The day earlier we knew nothing of this machine and would have bought the first one had they shown us the features *we* wanted, not the features *they* wanted to show.

Stick to their needs

When your people are selling, are they wasting their time? Are they doing a 'letter perfect' demonstration that follows a standard procedure, forgetting about what the customers needs?

Are they fooling themselves? Oscar Wilde, the playwright and wit, put it amusingly. Upon arriving at his English club after seeing one of his plays which had failed to please the audience, he was asked by a friend, 'How was it?' Wilde replied, 'The play was a great success, but the audience was a failure.' Do we kid ourselves into thinking our failure is the customer's fault?

In order to profit, every salesperson must find out what customers want and concentrate only on those needs. We only have 17 minutes in which to hold a person's attention in face-to-face meetings.

Do we want to waste those 17 minutes or should we use that valuable time to discuss their needs? Shouldn't we find out which benefits interest them? To be successful we must stick to their needs, and nothing else.

Just ask!

How do we find out what the customer's needs are? The best way is to ask them! This is true of many things in life, not just sales. I remember hearing about a psychologist who had cured many people suffering from schizophrenia. These were people whom institutes had deemed completely incurable.

Her patients, after their cure, moved on to become valuable members of society, as lawyers, academics—highly educated and successful people. What was the incredible secret of her success? Among the complexities of her system was one basic premise. She asked them what they needed!

Had they been mistreated when they were three years old, or six? What had they missed in life? Love, attention, encouragement? She asked them what they needed and they told her.

No one else had thought of that—of asking those people what they needed. Yet their answers revolutionized the results which were achieved.

Have your people thought of asking their customers what they need? Perhaps if they ask more often, and concentrate only on those needs, they will revolutionize their results!

B	B	B	B	B	B	B	B	B
1	2	3	4	5	6	7	8	9
		X			X	X		

B = Benefits of your product/service
X = Those benefits you have decided to emphasize and explain after asking probing questions to determine the needs.

- Remember that the human attention span is limited. Some research shows that we only have 17 minutes in face-to-face presentations and as little as 2 minutes on the telephone to make an impact. Therefore we must probe effectively to find out which benefit the customer wants.

- Don't wait for the customers to tell you which benefit(s) they want; ask them!

- By asking them, you won't run the risk of jumping to conclusions and your presentation will be in line with their needs.

- By asking them what is important, you will reinforce their own thinking about their needs, make their decision process clearer and quicker, and help them to prioritize their needs.

Figure 2   Identifying the benefits that are most important to each customer

The principle of asking is simple, it's basic and it's critical to success in anything we do.

How often do we really ask people what they need?

Listen!

Do we know what our husband or our wife wants from our marriage, or do we presume we know? Do we presume it's the same as we want or our parents wanted? Perhaps if we ask, we'll be surprised.

Perhaps we're like the two wordprocessor salespeople, so busy presuming we know what the other person wants that we don't hear the needs even when they stare us right in the face.

If it's true in personal life, surely it's true in business. If we're going to discover people's needs, we have to look and *listen*. We have to stop presuming we know.

Reconfirm that the benefits are right

Finally, when we do find out what the needs are, we have to prove we can meet those needs. We concentrate on the benefits which meet those needs until the benefits are crystal clear to the customer.

We have to confirm and reconfirm that the benefits are right. When we do that, the customer doesn't need to be sold to. When the benefits are right, and crystal clear, when the benefits match their needs, they buy.

Remember, to Make Buying Easy:

Don't sell. Clear the path so they can buy.

Review of Part Three

Basic Techniques
to Make Buying Easy

Chapter 6   Help the Customers to Recognize Their Needs

1. Get the Customers to Verbalize Needs
2. Probe for Needs with Questions
3. Get the Need or Lose the Sale

Chapter 7   Don't Sell—Let Them Buy

1. Identify the Benefits Which are Most Important to Each Customer
2. Stick to Their Needs
3. Just Ask!
4. Listen
5. Reconfirm that the Benefits are Right

Part III Action Sheet

Ideas for Development:

- Become proficient at asking questions to reinforce the customer's buying motive
- Identify the benefits which are most important and stick to them
-
-
-
-
-
-

Of the above ideas, which one is likely to yield the best results?

What percentage of sales (or performance) increase could realistically be expected?

How long would it take:
    to develop the idea?
    to get results?

Who would have to be involved?

What date should we start?

What is the first step I should take?

PART FOUR
How To Break The Objection Barrier

8

If You Do This
You'll Never Worry about Objections

An objection is like smoke; if its not cleared, it lingers.

Why are objections often a nightmare to the sales force? The answer is simple.

Adopt a positive attitude

Most people dread objections rather than welcoming them. So to deal effectively with objections, the first step is to change our attitude.

In order to do that, think about this. Would anyone buy a product without having some questions and concerns about it? Let's put ourselves in the place of the prospect and remember the last time we bought something. The decision cycle works through a questioning process. We all take in new facts, process them, ask questions or wonder silently, listen and look, and then, piece by piece, come to a decision.

Therefore, the objection process is a normal part of the buying cycle. If prospects have no questions or objections, they probably have no interest. Since that's the case, why not welcome objections? In fact, theoretically, the more questions and objections, the more interest there is. No one asks questions when they're not interested.

Why not think of objections as an integral part of the whole sales process? It's something to work with from beginning to end. The fact is that the whole sales process is an objection-encountering process.

If we become comfortable with this fact, then we can develop the most effective methods of dealing with it.

Hit objections head on

Ignoring objections can be fatal! We can't try to ignore objections. If we ignore the prospects' concern, we are *discounting* their needs. No one likes to be ignored. We must hear the concern and acknowledge it in such a way that the prospect knows we've heard it.

Would we continue to see a doctor if every time we mentioned a problem, he ignored it and kept talking about something else? Of course not.

The same is true in selling. We must listen and recognize the objection, then work with the customer to clarify the issue if we are to build their commitment.

Do you find in your businesses that there are certain objections which are brought out repeatedly in each selling situation? For most companies this is true. They each have objections peculiar to their business. They get better results if they hit the objection head on. They actually bring up the subject before the prospects does.

This is an excellent system because it puts the prospect's mind at ease. It's comforting to know that the objection has been dealt with and overcome before with other customers. By bringing up the objection first, and proving you've dealt with it, you let the prospect know that you are truly interested in the welfare of your customers. That builds trust, and trust builds a relationship which succeeds.

Recognize three forms of objections

To become adept at working with objections we need to be able to recognize them.

Objections take three forms: questions, statements and last, but not least, your own feeling about the prospect's uneasiness or uncertainty. Here are three examples.

Questions

Let us say a prospect is taking a tour of your factory. When talking about how your products are stocked, the prospect asks 'How much of your work is off-the-shelf and how much is built to specification?'

Statements

Or he makes a statement, 'Most of our suppliers deliver within seven days of our order. I presume you do this too.'

Actions

Or he says nothing, but when passing through your factory with you, pauses at one particular production stage. You wonder why. Perhaps he has a negative impression which is wrong. If you ask, you can clear up the doubt immediately. If you let it go, the bad impression will stick and it will linger forever like smoke.

Ask 'why do you ask?'

Regardless of how the objection is brought to your attention, you need to probe to get to the bottom of the matter. In the three examples above, what are the prospects really asking? All three may be asking themselves if you can meet their delivery requirements.

In the first question about 'off-the-shelf versus specification work', they may fear that you spend so much time on specials that you won't have stock built up when they need it. You need to find out the reasons for questions. 'Why do you ask?'

If they have the wrong impression, you can correct it. If they have the right impression, you can reinforce it. 'Oh, yes, we always have stock on hand.'

In the next example, the customer makes a statement about their customary seven-day delivery from suppliers. They are probably looking for an acknowledgement from you that you can match or better this.

Here's your chance to push a benefit and make it come alive with a story. If you can deliver in three days, you'll want to let them know and give them an example for reassurance.

'Yes, in fact we pride ourselves on our prompt delivery capability. Just recently, Jim Smith, our client across the road, called our production director to thank him for getting him out of a tight spot. He ran low on supply and we got him a delivery within the day. This kept his production line going, and of course he appreciates our efforts.'

Then tell him what you'll do for him. 'Our normal practice is three-day delivery.' Then you'll want to follow up with a confirming question. 'Would that be important to you in working with us?'

In the third example, the prospect pauses at one production point without commenting. You, of course, sense the prospect's uneasiness and probe to see what's on their mind. You might say, 'Is that similar to other processes you've seen?', or another question to open the conversation. Your purpose is to uncover the real doubt or fear.

If you discover they're worried about a bottleneck in production possibly leading to late deliveries, you can put their minds at ease and turn the subject into a benefit by citing a good example.

It will answer any doubts, and clear up the objection so that it doesn't linger.

To improve your sales effectiveness find out the reasons for people asking questions and making statements. Watch their behaviour. When you pick up non-verbal messages you'll be amazed what you discover. What you learn can change your life.

Focus your energy in any two-hour period each day over the next week to really look, listen and ask. Do two hours at work one week, then two hours at home. You'll be surprised at the increase in communication, at the raised understanding of people and their needs, and, most important, at your own satisfaction from these dealings.

Too often we presume we know. When we really look, listen and ask, we find out differently.

There are many ways that people communicate their feelings and objections. The way they act is as important as the words they use. Don't miss it.

And, don't forget to ask questions. In their best-selling book on principled negotiation, *Getting to Yes*, Roger Fisher and William Ury talk about the importance of finding out people's interests and reasons before negotiating. That way the results can meet everyone's needs. Fisher and Ury believe everyone should benefit. If this method of asking questions is beneficial to high-power negotiations, then it can be beneficial to us in our sales development.

Remember, To Break the Objection Barrier:

**Never Worry About Objections:
Hit Them Head-On.**

---

[1] Roger Fisher and William Ury, *Getting to Yes* (New York, Penguin Books, 1983), pp. 41–57.

9

A Three-Step Formula
for Turning Objections into Approvals

There's one critical thing that many people in sales overlook. That is the fact that the buyer *must* feel that we hear and understand their objection. This is imperative. If they don't, all the logical and effective arguments in the world won't convince them. We must *prove* we hear. This we call 'cushioning the objection', or showing our sympathy.

In our seminars, we use a very effective, three-step formula for turning objections into approvals. It's simple, easy, and if carried out properly, gets tremendous results. When a customer has an objection, do this:

- The Cushioning Segment
- The Explanatory Segment
- The Close Off or Recycle Segment

Remember, to break the objection barrier use the three-step formula.

The amount of time we give each segment depends on the complexity and severity of the objection.

A mild objection could be handled by combining all three segments in just a sentence or two.

A severe objection could require a long period of time for each segment. The important thing is to go through all three steps on *each* and *every* objection.

Let's look at some actual examples. In our business prospective clients sometimes wonder how we can help them without having technical knowledge of their product. They sometimes say, 'I like the practical approach of your service, but I wonder how you can help without knowing about the technical aspects of our business.'

Show, talk and prove your concern

The first step is the cushion. Show understanding. 'Yes, Mr Jones I can certainly understand your concern.'

Don't stop there; this is a serious objection, fundamental to the whole discussion. 'In fact, this is the same concern that most other clients have the first time they come to see us.' Here you're showing Mr Jones that you not only understand, you're even open enough to agree that others have the same concern.

You're now starting to be reliable in his eyes. At the same time, you're giving him a positive indication that the problem can be solved by using the term 'most other clients'. You wouldn't have clients if the problem couldn't be solved.

You continue, 'I know that you must have this point absolutely clarified or you won't be confident about our service.'

Now you're further agreeing with his concern and starting to link his concern with an explanation by saying he must have the point clarified. This puts him in a receptive frame of mind to receive the explanation, providing you've done enough cushioning to suit his personality and the severity of the objection.

If you don't do this step, you're lost. Why? Because, without a cushion, the explanations bounce back as if they were arrows hitting a brick wall. An explanation will never penetrate the buyer's mind if the objection isn't cleared first.

There's a straightforward reason for this. Part of the buyer's mind is still distracted by doubt. The doubt causes a mental shield to go up. Most of your explanation can't penetrate the shield because the buyer's mind is taken up with the objection.

You have to *prove* you hear and understand the objection, or your explanation falls on deaf ears. When you do prove to the buyer that you understand, the shield starts to disintegrate, allowing your explanations to penetrate. Eventually, the shield breaks down completely if your cushion and explanation are sufficient. If they're not sufficient, you have to start all over again. You cushion again and explain again.

Explain the reasons

When you've done enough cushioning, you move on the explanation. 'I mentioned earlier that we combine our commercial expertise with your company's technical expertise. Of course, in order to do this we need to understand all the key factors which influence our client's overseas sales. This includes the product features and benefits, the management policies, the competition, pricing and so on. Otherwise we couldn't do our job.'

This has two components. In the first part you're starting the explanation. In the last sentence you're cushioning again, agreeing that his concern is valid. If you didn't understand his company, you couldn't do the job.

Now you want to continue the explanation, and start to let Mr Jones see the benefits of working with you. This will move you closer to getting his approval.

'Most of our clients have been running their companies at least 10 years or even more. We can't learn everything they know, but we need to learn as much as possible in a short time. So, when we start working with clients we go out to them for an intensive briefing session.'

Now, still in the explanation stage, you want to confirm that the message is getting through and start to build consensus. This is a good time for a question or two.

'Can you see how that works?' Then you might want to produce some evidence. Remember that a picture is worth a thousand words and will stay in the memory longer. He will forget 80% of what you tell him within two days.

'If we decide to work together, we come up to your premises and talk with you in depth. Some clients tell us that the questions we ask, plus the analysis we do, gives them new food for thought. Often they say that we ask them questions that they haven't asked themselves and that the analysis is useful to them for their domestic marketing as well as for the work we do with them overseas.' Now you're giving him a mental picture of how it works, and the extra benefits he can get.

'Mr Jones, would you like to see one of our briefing questionnaires? We usually telex it or send it to clients a week before the meeting so that they can prepare for it ahead. This means they can decide on the issues, gather the facts and figures and so on. Would it help you to look at it?' If he says no, he's probably satisfied. If yes, he's either still sceptical or really interested. Continue until you find out.

Ask if the concern is satisfied

That's the reason for the next step. We must clarify that the prospect is satisfied or not satisfied, by moving into the close-off or recycle segment. 'Does that satisfy your concern about how we work with clients effectively without previously knowing about their business?'

If you get an emphatic yes and you're satisfied that he is sure, you can consider it closed.

If you get a 'yes, but,' you recycle all three steps, the cushion, the explanation, and the close off. Start with the cushion, again. You probe more deeply into his concern once more, just as you did at first, so that you can provide a more appropriate cushion.

Since he's not satisfied, you know that either your cushion or your explanation was not satisfactory to him. So start with the cushion.

If you go straight to more explanation, as most people tend to do, you'll run the risk of losing the sale. Going back to the cushion never hurts and always helps.

Even if your problem is in the factual part of the explanation, going back to the cushion will satisfy his human need to be heard and valued for his concerns. After you cushion his concern—proving beyond a shadow of a doubt that you understand his objection and reason for the objection—then you can go on to the explanation.

In the explanation segment, you tell him why the product is the way it is. You tell him the benefits. Perhaps you can't overcome his objection, but you can offer alternatives. Perhaps the alternatives will make up a better package than he expected and overcome the objection.

Then you move again into the close-off segment. 'Does that answer your question?' Or, 'Does that satisfy your concern?'

When people object, there's always a reason. Find out why. Be concerned. Then you're free to move onto the explanation, the benefits and the order!

Remember, To break the Objection Barrier:

Start by Proving you Understand the Objection.

Review of Part Four

How to Break the Objection Barrier

Chapter 8   If You Do This, You Will Never Worry About Objections

1. Adopt a Positive Attitude
2. Hit Objections Head On
3. Recognize Them
      Questions
      Statements
      Your Own Feelings
4. Ask, 'Why Do You Ask?'

Chapter 9   A Three-Step Formula for Turning Objections into Approvals

1. Show, Talk and Prove Your Concern
2. Explain the Reasons
3. Ask if the Concern is Satisfied

Part IV Action Sheet

Ideas for Development:

- Hit objections head on
- Prove understanding of the objections
-
-
-
-
-
-

Of the above ideas, which one is likely to yield the best results?

What percentage of sales (or performance) increase could realistically be expected?

How long would it take:
    to develop the idea?
    to get results?

Who would have to be involved?

What date should we start?

What is the first step I should take?

PART FIVE

Six Ways To Stop Losing Business Needlessly

10

Why is 75% of All Business Lost on a Customer's First Contact with a Company?

Yes, its true, statistics prove that 75% of all business is lost on a customer's first contact with companies. Who is responsible for this?

The answer is straightforward. It's *anyone* ever having, at *anytime, any* contact with *any customer* or any buyer.

One of our clients, Ian McCallum, says 'I like to make everybody in my company think of themselves as involved in a sales organization. 'The time has gone,' says Ian, 'when any manufacturer like ourselves can afford to think of themselves as only manufacturing.'

Ian has an important point. Everyone in a company should realize that without customers there is no business. But how many people do? If they did, would 75% of our potential business be lost?

Who's responsible? We've already said everone's responsible who has contact with our customers and buyers. Does this include the receptionist, the service department, people in production, finance and so on?

In our sales and sales management seminars, we work with the attendees to determine which employees, in which departments, influence sales. When people realize how much potential business is lost by non-sales personnel, some real changes start taking place in organizations. They learn ways to develop harmony between departments and ways to motivate everyone to think of the customer as an integral part of their job. People start to realize that their livelihood depends on gaining and keeping customers.

If we're going to find out exactly where 75% of business is lost in our own companies, we have to look under every stone. We have to be openminded and look at our companies through new eyes—the eyes of the buyers.

Beware—contact points are critical

We have to look at every department, their practices and their people. Of all the 'contact points'—those having customer and buyer contact— we'll probably find that the 80/20 rule applies.

That narrows down our task. No doubt the 20% of our people having customer contact will have 80% of the influence. We can start there.

Who are they? Every company has a first contact point. That is a good place to start. Is it the switchboard operator or the receptionist perhaps?

Gordon Watson of McCall Associates told me about a talk he gave once to a retailers' meeting. He asked the group, 'Who do you think is the most important person in your company? Is it the Managing Director or the President?'

Then he went on and asked the group to visualize a pyramid. At the top of the pyramid sat the head of the company. Yes, he was important.

Under him, in the next level of the pyramid, sat the directors, the next level the senior managers, then more levels of managers, then the supervisors.

Then, all the layers forming the foundation of the pyramid were the members of staff. At the very cornerstone of the pyramid sat the receptionist or the switchboard operator. That person and that person alone was the customer's contact.

The customer doesn't know the people at the top of the pyramid. To them all that matters is their contact point—that's the most important person.

How many companies regard their switchboard operator as their most important person?

Ian McCallum and I were discussing his philosophy of training his people at Critchley to respond as a sales organization. He said he noticed that other companies sometimes bring in temporary help. The first place they seem to put the 'temp' is on reception or the switchboard.

How can new people on their first day on the job carry out the most important function in the company?

Try as they might, they can't possibly know all the people in the company in order to handle incoming calls effectively. They can't possibly know the products, or the customers.

If we want to stop losing business, we have to concentrate on contact points. Which are yours? When you identify them, you can start to take action to train and motivate them to win business and not lose it.

To make a dramatic increase in business, make a list of possible ways business is lost in your company. Then be persistant and inventive about changing it.

Dave Goillon was determined to take action. Dave owns a company called Acron, which manufactures equipment for the broadcasting industry and closed circuit TV. He became conscious of the importance of the customer's first impression and decided to take some quick and effective action.

What should be done, he wondered? Previously he had success with training films and so he found one which focused on answering the telephone. The effect of showing it brought excellent results. First he made it available only to the receptionist and secretaries.

They caught onto the idea that customers shouldn't be made to wait long periods while phones ring. They made up a sign for reception which said 'Three Rings'. Soon everyone was asking what the sign meant. They liked the idea and decided it was good sense not to keep customers waiting, even between departments when their call is transferred.

If you walk into Acron's manufacturing facility, you'll see people in every department—not just sales, but also service, testing, and so on—answering their phone before three rings. Do you think this kind of responsiveness leads to more business? Dave and his people are sure it does. Their 'three ring' motto keeps the customer in the forefront of their mind.

It shows what can be done with a little time and forethought to the problem. Dave took action to get his people trained and motivated. He got results.

Take responsibility for employee performance

A few years ago, during one of our recessionary times, I wrote a letter to the Editor of the *Financial Times* in London. In it I said, 'Isn't it up to management to take responsibility for the attitude and skill of their people?'

Some managers contend that employees have no concept of how their job relates to customers, to the business of the company and to the economy in general, and *can't be taught*.

I disagree. In my letter, I said, 'Isn't it time we take our head out of the sand and bring people into line with economic reality?' Bad business practices bring less business and less business brings fewer jobs. 'If we want our corporate world to survive, let's stop making excuses for people's performance and start taking responsibility.'

From the response which flowed in after the editorial letter was printed, I know others agree with me. Now is the time for action. Jim Kearn, who has run both American and British companies believes: 'Words don't mean anything, unless we do something'.

Let's all be sure we do something to identify the places where business is being lost and take steps to correct it. Let's not take the attitude that some managers have, that people can't be enlightened.

Attitudes—some need to be changed

I remember one day sitting in a university classroom when the business class professor told us a story. 'See that row of 20 apartment buildings across the street? There are 12 apartments in each building.

'The owner of those buildings hasn't paid income tax for the last nine years! Not a penny!' Gasps came from everyone. 'Imagine, a rich person like that not paying income tax.' It confirmed the suspicions of most of us in the room who were non-capitalists at that stage of our life. We thought, 'Yes, capitalists are indeed villains, leaving the rest of us to pay taxes who could ill afford it by comparison.'

Next the professor said, 'I know that man. He started with only $100 years ago when he bought his first apartment. He borrowed the downpayment from family and friends. Then he worked at two jobs— one, during the day, the other at night to pay off his debt. At week-ends he worked to paint and repair the buildings. The first few years were really blood, sweat and tears. Gradually he made enough money to buy another building and another.

'Due to his hard work and his willingness to risk his capital, he has provided housing and jobs for hundreds of people. Because of his policy of keeping his property in top-notch condition, there were jobs created for painters, plumbers, gardeners and electricians. His apartments are also creating a demand for supplies: carpets, curtains, kitchen applian-ces and so on which are creating other businesses and more jobs. Where would we be without people who were willing to take these risks to keep money and jobs in circulation? In addition, he pays taxes on all products and services he buys.'

There you have it. I suddenly had a new perspective on capitalism. It changed my thinking from that point on. The change came from the vivid step-by-step understanding of the process of job creation and money circulation.

We know that perspectives can be changed. People usually just need someone to enlighten them. Otherwise they carry around preconceived ideas which go unexamined until someone gives them new facts which change the way they look at things. But the enlightenment has to come in a way which they personally find logical, not as take-it-or-leave-it facts. We all know that from our own past experience.

If the professor hadn't used the step-by-step process and instead said, 'People with money create jobs, you should support them', what do you think our level of acceptance would be? You're right; zero—because we wouldn't have built up our own mental picture of the links in the chain of the process. Instead we'd hold to our old picture—the preconceived idea which didn't link wealth and job creation together.

The point is that employees who don't link their own job to the value of the customer haven't been enlightened. And they are not going to change their idea because some manager comes in and says to them, 'You must stop coming in five minutes late in the morning. Think of all the customer calls you're missing.' It doesn't make a link with them.

They have to be made to understand that without customers, there is no company, and without a company, there are no jobs including their own.

If you can turn someone from a non-capitalist to a capitalist with one easy story, think what results you can get when you make employees understand the value of the customer.

Someone has to take the time to sit down and explain the process of job creation or whatever else it is they need to understand the value of the customer better. Otherwise people continue with preconceived ideas. It's our responsibility as managers to make sure they understand the value of the customer and handle their job effectively.

When Gordon Watson was addressing the retailers' association about the importance of the customer's first contact, what do you think he had in mind about the way people should be treated?

Let's take the most successful companies. What do the heads of those companies, sitting at the top of the pyramid, believe about the ways customers should be treated? What's the common thread which makes them successful?

Think of the companies you most like dealing with and you'll know the answer. Chances are that your requests are treated with care and concern. Besides offering a good product, the companies pay attention to human needs. They treat you with the courtesy and respect that good customers deserve.

If, on the other hand, you deal with a company whose employees take an offhand approach to you and your needs, you'll probably go somewhere else.

When I think of exceptional service, I think of my printer, Chris Marson, in Reading. I remember meeting him on a Sunday many years ago to review some proofs. Although his back was out, he kept his date and came to the appointment with a painful limp. His service has always been impeccable. Even though his printing presses are running seven days a week and Chris never has a spare moment, he always makes time to come to the phone with a friendly, 'Hello, Christine, how are you, all right? Good to hear from you', and his voice says he means it. He knows that price and service are essential but not everything. He knows the value of the human factor.

Concentrate on the human factor

What areas of your business require attention to 'the human factor' in dealing with your customers? If you concentrate your thoughts on this, you'll develop ideas which relate to your buyers. You'll retain some of that 75% of potential business that slips away.

Here's an example of what we did at Intrinsic Marketing. At one point we analysed our operation and decided that not enough personal attention was being given to prospective clients at their first visit to us. Since we were in a serviced office building at the time, we had no control over the reception area. Sometimes visitors were greeted professionally and sometimes not, depending on who was on duty. We knew that the first few minutes the prospects waited, were critical to their lasting judgement of us.

We had to take drastic action. We put together a two-part plan which at the time seemed a little 'over the top'. But we had to try something.

Here's what we did to overcome the questionable reception. First we called visitors several days before the meeting to confirm the appointment and we did one more thing to give it a personal touch. 'Mr Jones, we're looking forward to seeing you on Tuesday at 3.00. By the way, we like to have everyone's coffee ready when they arrive, how do you like yours?'

The results were very good. We had previously worried that people would think this was silly, but they didn't. They liked the personal touch. They even commented on how nice it was to work with people who took the time and trouble over personal details.

The second part of our new policy was to go out into the reception area *immediately* upon their arrival. If the conference room wasn't ready, we chatted with them for a few minutes in reception while it was being prepared. Again, the results were remarkable. People liked being personally attended to. They also had no time to focus on the reception.

It proved to pay off handsomely—our conversion of prospects to clients went up immediately. Furthermore, the new clients started to openly talk to us about the procedures.

They told us how impressed they were with the way we handled our business. They thought it was 'marketing at its best'. Ian McCallum, a client of ours, was one of the people who visited us during that time. He said he liked 'Everything from the sales presentation to the smallest personal detail—even our attention to how people like their coffee.' It taught us a lesson. We now know how important the human factor is. We also know that sometimes you have to be inventive to solve human factor problems.

The human factor is important in every business. Some people use it instinctively, and therefore are tremendously successful in business. Others don't, and they lose business needlessly despite having superior products or services. Watch the way you're treated the next time you buy something. It will give you a wealth of ideas on 'how to' and 'how not to' treat customers.

All companies have areas in which the human factor can be improved. What areas are these in your company? If you identify these, and give them creative solutions, you'll prevent business from being lost needlessly. If you're thinking about new ways to generate business, think about this one. When you stop losing business, you are in effect creating a new way to generate business.

Remember, to Stop Losing Business Needlessly:

Regain the Lost 75% of Sales—Make Everyone Responsible for Sales

11

Successful Interface Between Sales, Finance, Production and Service —Is It Essential?

A trade delegation from the Far East not long ago visited a factory in the Washington DC area. They had a total expenditure budget of 25 million dollars. They wanted to visit companies and were ready to sign on the dotted line to order the equipment they needed.

The state commercial officer who was co-ordinating their visit, called one factory to arrange a visit for the next day. He informed them that the delegation wanted machinery demonstrations.

The next day the delegation duly arrived. They were greeted by the Production Director and given a demonstration. There was no one from the sales department on hand to assist. The delegates were impressed and several were ready to place their orders. But, would you believe, they were told by the Production Director that there was no one to finalize sales details. They moved on to a competitor's factory and placed their order there!

'What happened to the internal communication of the first factory?' Bill and I asked in amazement, as we talked with the state officer who relayed the story to us. 'Well, the production department heard that the delegation wanted a demonstration tour and nobody at the company thought they were coming to buy!' he said. As a result they lost a $500,000 worth of sales.

This true story exemplifies how easy it is for people, including key employees, to lose sight of the fact that they are in business to sell.

The three vital questions to be asked of ourselves are:

- Are all our people trained to recognize a sales enquiry?
- Do we have a way of alerting sales teams of sudden important enquiries so that sales can take place?

- Do other directors in the company have the authority to finalize sales when necessary?

If this had been the case with the above company they would be half a million dollars richer today. Therefore maintaining sales through a good interface between departments is essential. What steps can you take to improve the link?

Very often in our seminars on developing effective sales we have a wide range of staff members, not just sales. Some come from production, some from finance and so on. They learn, alongside sales managers and sales staff, how other departments can win and lose business. The results are enlightening.

Overcome resistence to selling

It's not easy to make everyone in the company feel they are in business to sell. Yet, as we discussed in the last chapter, the more progressive companies are doing just that—and making a success of it.

Let's take one of the most unlikely professions we can think of as relating to sales. How about banking. Several years ago I was lecturing to a group of bank branch managers in Northern England, and the area manager who was in charge of 24 branches told me his secret of success.

'Every month I get my branch managers together and I tell them to remember that they are salesmen', he said. 'With over 50 different services to offer, and customers to keep happy, they cannot afford to think of themselves as anything else.'

If taking a sales orientation works in banking, surely it can be applied in all industries.

Robert Louis Stevenson said in the late 1800s, 'Everyone lives by selling something.' Managers can create attitude changes so that effective training can take place. It's not an easy job, but who said success comes easily?

Will you run into resistance from employees who don't believe their job relates to sales? Dave Goillon at Acron found resistance from his engineers when it came to sales training. Even though technical inquiries came directly to them, they didn't feel that sales related to them. Dave tried to entice them by offering a training film designed for non-sales personnel, but they weren't convinced they needed it.

Dave considered his options. 'I could have forced it on them, but I knew I needed their co-operation. Since the video unit was in their area, I decided to show it to another group and let the engineers just observe.'

It wasn't long before the engineers were requesting a showing of their own. Dave used the principle that there's nothing worse than feeling left out of training.

If others are learning something useful, everyone wants their share. By creating an eager want, he got results when a direct approach failed. He achieved the training that was needed.

The engineers now keep a log by the phone to record every prospect's name, phone number and enquiry. Dave estimates that a substantial increase in sales now occurs because of the improved image the customer has of the company, as well as the improved tracking system made possible by keeping record of the phone calls as they come in. Awareness and training has paid off.

Improve the relationships between departments

Small companies we work with think that their interface between departments is more difficult than with big companies. Not so, we tell them. Here's proof.

In 1981, Judith Leeming, the scholarship recipient of an award programme I run called 'The Most Promising Young Businesswomen', did a sales internship which we arranged with a leading FORTUNE 500 company. This company had a fine reputation for high quality office equipment. They had a superb sales training programme, recognized internationally.

Judith spent three weeks with them, first having theoretical sales training and then time with sales people on the road. As a follow-up she spent a week in an after-sales department, where delivery schedules were implemented. 'Much to my amazement', Judith said, 'I discovered that the service department had no idea how difficult sales were to achieve. In fact, they often treated new sales indifferently. They paid little attention to delivery schedules and didn't realize how easily they could lose sales!'

They placed little care on communicating with the sales department if there were outstanding questions relating to the paperwork. They failed to recognize that a sale could be jeapordized by delay or indifference. The whole sales effort seemed to dissolve in importance.

After graduation from university, Judith interviewed for many high-powered jobs. The interviewers were intrigued with her sales internship and asked what important lessons she learned. Her answer: 'The importance of good liaison between sales and other departments. To have a good sales department is not enough.' Her insight landed her a prestigious position in international banking, marketing its services to aerospace industries. Later she was transferred to Singapore and held one of the top positions in the Far East region with her organization. Her lesson served her well.

Jim Kearns has proved the value of getting internal support to ensure sales collaboration from all departments. He believes that awareness brings understanding, and that understanding brings co-operation. He's developed a unique and effective way of bringing it about.

While heading the International Division of his company, Jim has taken sales of their products in the US from $150,000 to $15,000,000 between 1978 and 1985.

To build a solid base for his expansion, Jim knew he had to build everyone's awareness of sales in order to get their co-operation. Only with this co-operation between departments could he continue to dramatically increase sales.

Here's what Jim told me. 'On the last Friday of every month I run a sales meeting for my department. At that meeting we have what we call 'Highlights and Lowlights'. Everyone informally tells about the highlights—the goals that were met, and the lowlights—the goals that still need attention.'

There are no notes other than the secretary's and no formal paperwork. 'Everyone is relaxed and the atmosphere is supportive.' Jim is careful to bring up sensitive subjects such as incomplete goals in a casual, supportive way. 'I want to give confidence to those involved that they can accomplish their goals.' this subtlety, he finds, makes people want to use their full skills and effort to reach their goals.

But Jim doesn't end his co-operative campaign there with only his department! He invites other key department employees to join in after the internal proceedings have finished.

'The Friday meeting starts about 4.00 and runs until about 5.30. Then we invite guests from other departments. This gives the International Division a chance to recount successes and explain the needs and expectation for the future.'

The value is twofold. Firstly it provides vital awareness, understanding and support from other departments. Secondly it provides the equally important communication and motivation within his department. Now Jim's department gets support from other departments in a way that far surpasses formal meetings of any kind.

When I talked with Jim about his secrets of success, it seemed to me that there was a lot more planning behind these meetings than met the eye. Was it really a casual, impromptu evening where everyone spoke off the cuff? Perhaps not. Jim's people know he has high expectations of them and they see the Friday meetings as an important time to acknowledge their successes ....

Does Jim run the meeting off the cuff, with no notes? No. He's careful to review the notes before each meeting, so that he can bring up unresolved issues or give credit where it's due.

Would your company benefit from a 100-fold increase in seven years as his company did?

Stuart Sanders, who is head of the Financial Futures company within Lloyds Bank, finds that he is able to improve the relationship between departments by acknowledging the value of the people behind the scenes.

'I never dismiss our back office people, because I know they are one of our biggest assets. They are the final link in the chain. If the final link is unsupportive or unco-operative, the customer can be lost. If this happens, all the effort leading up to that point is also lost.'

Stuart has found that sales training for his non front-liners has paid big dividends. It has opened their eyes to the problems of the sales force and the value of good customer relations.

Could you personally benefit from better interface between departments? Undoubtedly there are people in your workplace who influence your working style, your attitude, your job satisfaction. Are you waiting for them to take the first step? Are you waiting for them to improve the situation?

Why wait? It may never happen. Why not take the first step? At home, on the job, in the community. Let them see how their activities link to your activities. Let them see the areas of mutual interest and the gain to be had from better co-operation. Your reward will be immediate satisfaction. Why not make a greater effort now and see what results you get?

What steps can you take to increase the interface between departments? Look at every possibility. Be creative. The results will speak for themselves.

Remember, to Stop Losing Business Needlessly:

**Educate and Motivate All Departments
To Support Sales.**

12

The Lost Inquiry—
More Common Than You Think!

Does your company have an accountant? Most companies have someone in charge of keeping track of the money. The bigger the company, the more people they have keeping track.

But what about sales inquiries? Who keeps track of them? One person? Several people? No one?

Is there a system or a set of books to track inquiries just as we keep books to track money in and money out?

Imagine it—no company worth its salt would *not* have a system to track its money. Yet it often doesn't have systems for tracking sales inquiries.

Treat inquiries like gold

Isn't an inquiry as good as cash? Didn't you spend money to generate the inquiry? Perhaps you advertised and publicized your product. You spent years in product development to make sure you had the very best product possible for your customer. Yet, when it comes to the sales inquiry, do you treat it like gold? No, most don't even treat it as well as they treat cash.

With cash, every penny gets recorded. When one penny is missing, people want to know why. But what happens when an inquiry is missing. Usually no one notices. Probably, unlike money, there was no one responsible for tracking all the sales leads and inquiries coming in.

Perhaps the salespeople keep their own leads. If so, where do they keep them? In the safe, like money? No. More likely in the briefcase, the drawer, the filing cabinet, the car, the house, the jacket pocket. Not just one of those places, but all of those places.

Since we don't treat money like that, why should we treat leads—an equally important commodity—like that? Isn't it true that if our tracking system is less effective than our accounting system we cannot expect accuracy and reliability? It's certain that we are not getting the results we should.

There's more to tracking than meets the eye. In tracking the inquiry we should record:

- When it comes in
- When it should be acted upon
- When it was acted upon
- When it should next be acted upon
- When it turned into a sale or was rejected

Then there are categories of leads.

A good way to split up the leads in your mind is to think of two distinct groups of leads—the traditional and the untraditional leads.

On a flight from Boston to Tampa, I was talking to the district manager of a company which does demographic studies for fast food companies. The restaurants always use his service to project the growth in areas before opening a new site. We were discussing how he generates business and he told me they had a perfect system for keeping track of their sales inquiries. Every inquiry which is recorded is followed up diligently and on time.

Then he told me that half of their business was from referrals. 'Great', I said, 'how does a referred lead enter your system?'

'Oh', he said, 'no prospects actually enter our system unless they call in or write.' Then he paused and reflected, 'Oops', he said, 'now I see why you asked, half of our potential business is not being followed up because it doesn't enter the system!'

That's what I mean by untraditional leads.

Every company has some standard, traditional ways of generating business interest, and these we call the traditional leads. These could be advertising responses, direct mail responses, exhibition responses and so on.

Every company also has untraditional, non-standard ways it gets business. These we call the untraditional leads.

These could be leads gained as casually as meeting a prospective customer at a friend's house, a party, or while travelling. It could be referrals from others, a call-in, and so on. Much to a company's surprise they often find that very big sales are generated through these untraditional channels. Yet when an inquiry comes up, they don't necessarily put it into their system for follow-up. It often remains just a card in someone's pocket.

Develop an airtight tracking system

The point is that both categories can suffer from ineffective follow up if an airtight system is not developed.

If you already have a system, the question is, how airtight is it? Who is responsible for receiving the inquiry, for logging it, for acting on it initially, for following it up later? Who's responsible for monitoring all inquiries at each of the above stages? Where are the records kept for ease of management review?

How are the records kept? A tracking system which is both *easy to use* and *easy to monitor* is essential. It takes time and effort to develop. It usually needs modification as the company grows or develops new services. It must be developed by someone who understands and controls the departments which interface on the logging, action, follow up and so on. Otherwise, the system may not be compatible with each department.

Spot the weaknesses

Let's look at a company which is losing business needlessly due to weak tracking and follow up. Here's how it handles its business, step by step. Where do you see the weaknesses in the *wrong* methods they used?

— The company promotes its service through direct mail, sending letters, literature and reply cards to likely users.
— It attends one exhibition per year.
— It puts advertisements in journals which have reader-response cards, on a monthly basis.
— The mailing results in reply cards from interested parties on almost a daily basis.
— The sales managers distribute them to the sales force, according to territory, at the weekly sales meeting.
— The secretary logs the number of reply cards given to each.
— The sales force then calls each prospect to get an appointment.
— If successful, they mail product literature to them before the appointment.

— The salespeople keep their own records according to individual habits.
— The sales managers occasionally ask if the quality of the leads are good.
— The sales managers focus on the number of appointments each week, rather than on how the leads are being tracked or followed up.
— The managers feel that good sales people have a good system and don't need close monitoring.

What would you expect the lost business ratio to be for this company based on the management of inquiries as described above?

This company is losing a tremendous amount of its sales needlessly. Its average loss on the Harvey-Sykes scale is 60%!

If it stopped losing this business it could have a 150% increase in sales.

Let's look at this carefully because the company is spending a lot of money on what should be a sound lead generating system, but is losing it on the follow up.

The advertising and direct mail are sound because they are generating valid leads. But the follow up is weak.

Find the cure

What could it do to save the 60% lost business? Let's look at it from the top down. With its current system there is no uniformity in the way leads are handled. Therefore, there is no management control. When there is no management control, how can one plan growth for the future and actively control it?

The company needs a uniform tracking system which the sales manager or the head of the company can access on a regular basis. The system should record each attempt to contact the prospects, conversations held, visits, and so on.

If you're not in management, but you want to improve your own results, you can create your own system. Then you or the managers should have weekly activity reports showing the number of conversations actually held, the number of sales conversions to appointments, the number of sales plus the value of each new sale. Then they could judge consistency of effort and spot trouble areas before they become problems.

In the previous example to spot weaknesses, you may have noticed that their timing also leaves a lot to be desired. Perhaps they enjoy passing out leads at the sales meeting. But so what? It may liven up the meeting, or give the sales manager a sense of power, but it does nothing for sales efficiency.

The lead could be almost a week old before reaching the sales force. By that time it is probably stale. Then, when you consider the postage time and the time for the salespeople to reach the prospect by phone, you could be talking about a 14-day, or more, delay between the prospect sending the card and the contact. In 14 days customer interest could wain. They might have already bought from the competitor! The solution – shorten the timing between contacts whenever possible.

Why do they call prospects only after receiving reply cards? They could call every prospect three days after the mailing is received to explain their service in more depth. This would generate substantially more appointments. Some companies generate as much as eight times as many appointments using this system. Naturally this costs more due to telephone charges and staff time. A financial return against investment could easily be calculated to help them decide whether to call all or just those sending cards back.

The management strategy to cure this company of its 60% lost business ratio and create a 150% increase in sales should be:

- Cut the time for response to leads in half.
- Incorporate a daily tracking sheet listing all prospects. The sales force can use this as a working tool.
- Weekly follow-up calendars should be used by each member of the sales force to record those who need to be called.
- A weekly activity summary sheet should list calls and results.
- A similar results report with monthly totals should be developed.

Tracking systems are essential to management and salespeople alike. A good system once adopted is appreciated for the self discipline it imposes on everyone. It should be simple to work with and easy to understand by those who review it.

Put every lead into the system

Track exhibition and advertising leads

I remember watching a marketing manager come into the office after an exhibition. He reached into his pocket, pulled out a handful of business cards, and threw them on the sales secretary's desk. 'Ann, here's the exhibition leads', he said.

That's the way leads passed from marketing to sales. The secretary filed them away and two months later the sales manager attempted a follow-up plan. Most of the prospects had already spent their money elsewhere. This sad but true story too often repeats itself.

When advertising or an exhibition is done, leads are generated. The same tracking system can be used or a similar one developed. The important thing is that *each* inquiry enters the system and is followed up *quickly*.

Companies spend vast sums for exhibition stands, yet follow-up is often left to the discretion of each member of the salesforce. Many times salespeople are pressed for time due to sales commitments prior to and following the exhibition. Cards which are collected at exhibitions but never enter the system don't create sales.

Unless someone is specifically responsible for exhibition follow-up, this is exactly what can happen. Why not appoint someone from inside or outside the sales force to be responsible for getting the inquiries into the system? After all, the lead is as good as gold. Why not put someone in charge of it. Once in the system, the leads can be followed up in the normal way.

Track non-sales department leads

Another area of potential lost sales for companies is the inquiry picked up outside the sales department. It could be a telephone call-in picked up by the security guard, the passing production engineer, or the switchboard. Therefore, everyone in a company needs to become aware of the existence of the tracking system and the importance of getting the lead into the system.

But knowledge alone won't save leads. The best system we've seen is one in which a central person is designated as the lead 'co-ordinator'. This person can have the responsibility of entering leads into the system on a daily basis whether they come in by telephone, through production or on a scrap of paper from a cocktail party. All traditional and untraditional leads should go into the system.

Keep a phone log

Remember Dave Goillon's engineers who were mentioned earlier? Why not keep a jotting pad by the phone in every department to record names and phone numbers of prospects.

At Intrinsic we keep a phone 'call-in book' at each telephone. Later someone switches the relevant inquiry information to the tracking system. By recording each call we also get the spin-off benefit of being able to refer back to anyone who called, the date, their phone number and so on.

How effective is your lead tracking and conversion system, and how does it compare to those of other companies? Give yourself a 10 out of 10 *if*:

— You can immediately put your hands on a list of all traditional and untraditional inquiries in one place, kept for easy access and tracking — this can be one central place for each member of the sales team.

— All inquiries are duplicated in a master file for current and future reference.

— A calenderized tracking system records each future action for each prospect and the date it is to be taken.

— Management gets a regular breakdown of the activities and results of each member of the team.

— Management studies the activity details regularly and takes corrective action before problems occur.

If your systems aren't as airtight as you would like, don't despair. But take action now to correct it. The results might surprise you.

They surprised Phil Parker. He is on the sales desk of Financial Futures trading with Lloyds Merchant Bank. After coming on one of our seminars, the first action he took was to start a lead tracking system.

The course finished on June 7. On June 8, a colleague of Phil's gave him a lead. He called and found out that the prospect was on holiday but would be back on June 23. He entered the name into his new lead tracking system, with a check in the column for June 23. Then a series of conversations ensued, in fact nine carefully followed up phone calls over the next nine weeks. They were all duely noted in Phil's lead account book.

Suddenly in the tenth week, on September 8, exactly three months after his first call, Phil got a call. It was the prospect, this time calling Phil. He said, 'I'm ready to order.'

Without the system, Phil told me, he might have called once or twice, but over a three-month period the client would have been forgotten.

The important thing is that with a system like Phil's, *you are in control*. Your effort is documented and logged. You know exactly where you stand with each prospect.

What if someone in Phil's position had started 10, 20 or 50 clients, and after a few calls, given them up? There would be enormous wasted effort. Why not make your effort *really* count?

Now you have food for thought. The sooner you get an effective system, the sooner your results will increase.

Effective systems rely on three things:
First, the system
— it must be good and easy to use.
Second, the management of the system
— someone needs to co-ordinate and monitor the carry through.
Third, the lead co-ordinator
— one person needs to be responsible for putting leads into the system.

If you want to improve your own performance, independent of others, you will have to carry out all three tasks yourself. It will be worth it. You'll feel much more in control of your activities and your results will go up dramatically.

What if you're reading this book but you're not in sales?

The same system can be used for achieving any goal.

When Bill and I were collaborating on this book, I realized that we only had three months left to complete it. I wanted time to do four re-writes of each chapter. With 25 chapters and four re-writes, that meant 100 days were needed with only one day per chapter.

As three months only have 90 days, we were already pressed, not to mention time for translantic mail of the chapters back and forth. I solved the problem by reallocating the time, giving me more time for the first draft of each chapter, and less time for re-write touch ups. We made our deadline because I created a tracking system for what had to be done each day.

But I know why many people miss deadlines. If I hadn't applied my business knowledge and practised what I preached, I would have missed mine too. No matter what your goal is, use a tracking system. Know how much you have to accomplish each day.

Remember, to Stop Losing Business Needlessly:

Develop an airtight tracking system.

13

The Make or Break Buying Period

How long does it take for customers to decide whether or not to buy a product? In retail, a customer may make the decision to buy a cosmetic in three minutes. In aerospace the decision could take three years or more and involve several layers of decision making.

We call the time period between customer awareness of the product and their decision the critical 'make or break' buying period.

The reason that this period is critical is that we can make or break our chances of selling during that period by our actions.

What is the average buying decision period for your product? Every company has an average customer buying cycle. This period varies between industries.

Don't deny your customer buying cycle

I know many salespeople who deny that an average period can be determined. They reason that each customer is different and by denying there is a critical period, they put their energy into the sale too late. This weakens their effectiveness. They neglect to do the appropriate things while the customer's interest is the highest, and therefore lose the business. Instead they will concentrate energy on the period when customer interest is waining, causing frustration for themselves, their company and their customer. In fact, 80% of ineffective salespeople put their energy in at this stage. Don't let this happen to you and your people.

Figure 3 shows what we call the complete buying cycle.

Much of the success in selling our ideas or our product is, in fact, down to taking the right action at the right time.

Stage I. You'll see that Stage I is the period of the inquiry when the customer's interest starts to be enticed.

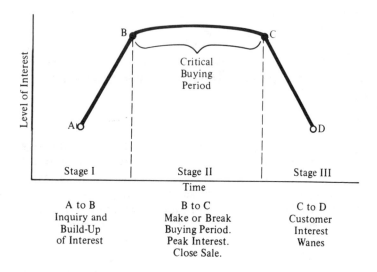

Figure 3   The customer buying cycle

Stage II.   During Stage II of the buying cycle the customer's interest is at its peak. This interest usually occurs during your presentation or the demonstration of the product. Sometimes it lasts until shortly afterwards. If we take the right action then, we will make the sale.

Stage III.   Customer's interest can only last so long. Other things can come in the way. Competitors can come along, doubts can build in their mind, or other priorities can come up. When interest starts to wane like this, we are in Stage III of the buying cycle.

Don't put your effort in too late

A top class salesperson or business executive—one who is respected for their success by their peers and community—knows that action needs to be taken when the time is right. In selling, they will put their emphasis at Stage II, when interest is at its peak. They know that they themselves must instigate the action and not wait.

However, it's easier to procrastinate, hoping problems will solve themselves, hoping sales will evolve by themselves. They don't, of course, and then people find themselves putting energy into the sale too late.

This kind of thinking is the sign of ineffectiveness. It's the sign of people not being honest with themselves. So we can say that self deception is the root of all evil, the root of losing business needlessly.

Why else do people not take appropriate action during the critical buying period? The three most common reasons are:

- Fear
- Insufficient methods
- Lack of management discipline or motivation.

If we have fear of answering objections during the presentation, the customers go away not fully understanding our product or services.

If we have fear of asking directly for a decision or commitment, it would be because we haven't developed a comfortable way of doing it. Then fear and insufficient methods both keep us from taking the right action at the right time.

The problem could be the lack of management skills. In this case even the best salespeople can periodically lose motivation.

Stop fear and improve your training methods

Let's take the case of fear of asking directly for a decision or commitment. This is an area which plagues most people, but can be easily overcome with a step-by-step questioning process.

Most people steer away from asking for the order because it sounds too direct. If the customer says, 'No,' it's too final. But we can ask for the order gradually without risk. The key is to work simply in small stages towards agreement.

I first became aware of the forcefulness of this process when a managing director complimented me for asking him, 'Does that look like the kind of thing you're looking for?'

Other simple questions serve the same purpose. We can all learn from each other and build up a repertoire of inoffensive and effective questions.

I remember listening to one of our own clients, Michael Campbell of Precision Chemicals, when, with his previous company, we were on a sales call in Cairo. After our introductions he opened his questioning by very simply asking. 'What would you be looking for from a supplier?' With that one simple question he was able to learn a tremendous amount about the customer's needs. This was the start of his closing process. Next, he went on to prove he could meet those needs.

A good opening question leads us easily to our close. For example, 'Mr Jones, earlier you mentioned you want reliability, quick delivery and a product which does X and X. Since ours offers these benefits and others, would you be able to add our name to the suppliers list?'

'When would the next request for quotation come up?'

'Do you have any requirements at the moment that we can satisfy?'

It's essential to increase our 'questioning' options for getting customer approval. This helps to overcome the fear people have of direct questioning.

Improve management discipline and motivation

What about management discipline and motivation as it relates to the critical buying period? Doesn't it make sense to keep our people focused on the 'critical buying period'? When we help them put their energy into Stage II, the peak buying period, they increase their returns. The company gains and they gain. Their motivation continues to go up, and so do their results.

Some companies keep their salespeople informed of the cost of sales development in order to demonstrate their support.

They record the costs, down to the penny of generating each lead, on each campaign they run. On direct mail, they calculate the cost of the envelope, the letter, the enclosures and response card.

Each week when the responses come in, all costs are added up and divided by the number of responses. The salesforce is told the cost per lead and this awareness keeps them more in tune with the support they are getting from the company. You can do this too.

They are made aware of the urgency of acting quickly in order to reinforce this expenditure. They realize that if the expenditure were stopped, the only alternative would be cold calling. The time and frustration needed to cold call takes valuable time away from face-to-face selling which means fewer sales.

If you want to put things more into perspective, you can allocate office overheads and marketing salaries to the cost per lead. If the first figure didn't impress them, this staggering one will! Don't forget to include the cost for brochure development and the cost of developing other promotional pieces in the packet.

The same costing process applies to advertising, exhibitions and so on. By telling the salesforce what it costs to run a sales department and the cost of a single lead, they can better understand the support system behind them.

If you have never done this exercise, the results will startle you. The true costs will probably be far greater than you anticipated. They will cause you to be sure that all sales activities are followed up during the critical buying period.

Knowing the cost of lead generation won't help everyone's motivation, but it won't hurt. You know your people and you know everyone needs to be motivated differently.

If you start to run a tighter ship, making sure that all sales people take action on closing the sale during the peak interest period—not a day later, not a week later, or a month later—then the success will bring your people the motivation to continue with good results. Success breeds success.

I always think of my good friend Lady Peggy Lindsay who makes her point about management practices more vivid by saying that 'Some efforts taken at the wrong time are as useless as pushing water uphill with a rake.' It's certainly true of efforts salespeople make during Stage II of the buying cycle. Putting effort into the close too late—by waiting until interest has started to wain—is like pushing water uphill with a rake!

Remember, to Stop Losing Business Needlessly:

**Don't Let Opportunities Slip Through Your Fingers.
Strike While The Iron Is Hot.**

14

How to Cure Follow-Up Complacency

Would anyone miss a sale purposely? Of course not.

Yet when any of us look back at the sales we've lost, it's easy to see what actions we should have taken. We could have acted faster, or we could have said something a better way. We blame ourselves or our sales team for not acting quickly and effectively.

Take preventative measures

Why not then take action ahead of time which will help to prevent us from slipping into this complacency mould next time? The real way to cure follow-up complacency is to carry out the sales process effectively at all stages. Then follow-up becomes less of a problem.

What is your sales closing ratio—that is, what percentage of business do you actually acquire from the total initial inquiries? Could you do better? If so, what would this increase mean to you personally, to your future, to your company?

In this chapter we'll show you three fool-proof, easy-to-use measures which can double, triple and quadruple your closing ratio. It's proven to work with companies of all sizes and all industries.

One problem with human nature is that we become comfortable with a new skill after we've mastered it. We learn to rely on it. We use it to the exclusion of all other potential skills or methods. Yes, we even become complacent. Why not break out of that mould?

Why not instead use our innate capability to acquire new skills? When we were children, we thought nothing of learning new skills each day. It became a habit.

We can recapture that habit if the *incentives* are high enough. And I don't mean monetary incentives. Everybody has their own incentives for learning and for peak performance. I was quoted in the leading economic magazine in Belgium, *Trends*, when this book came out in the

Dutch language as saying 'Money is not the top motivator.'

In surveys must people rate money as third in line as motivators. Other factors, differing for each person, job satisfaction, recognition, etc, take the number one and two places. What is your incentive for increasing your closing rate or the closing rate of your team?

Measure I—increase your options for putting your point across

With your incentive in mind let's look at nine options which we can train ourselves to use, and more importantly, which we should always come back to and improve in order to *continue* to increase our closing rate.

The following nine options, when practised, acquired and applied, give practical ways to express your ideas with impact and influence.

Paint a mental picture

Telling a story which involves the prospect—one in which they can see themselves using, benefiting and enjoying our product or service.

Let's say that we know from previous discussions that our prospect, John Jones, is under pressure to double the sales of his department next year and is thinking of using our seminars for in-house training.

So we might say, 'When you use our service we know you want to be sure you get immediate results. The way we help people get immediate results is to have them estimate the percentage increase in sales they will get from each section. They also make an implementation plan. This means they've taken the first step during the seminar.

'Imagine yourself as manager, being part of the planning process, with full commitment from your team.

'Imagine the feeling of confidence and control you'll have knowing each step which will be taken to reach each goal so that you can monitor the achievement and make policy adjustments as you go. You'll be able to sleep at night knowing exactly where you stand'.

He can then see himself using, benefiting and enjoying our service. What mental picture can you give about your product or service which incorporates these three points?

Use analogies

I once heard a man being interviewed on the radio who spent 15 minutes going from one analogy to the next.

Analogies take practice, but once you've mastered them they can be very effective. Practice by choosing any item in the room. Then tie it to your product, idea, or service. 'See that filing cabinet over there? In some ways it's like the steady, controlled growth you want for your company. You don't want to open the drawer one year and find it full, the next year empty. It's like the factory floor, you want it full at all times.' Practice analogies everywhere you go—in the car, while you walk, etc.

Show referral letters

Personalized referral letters which address specific issues are wonderful swayers of opinion, especially if they are genuinely honest and *specific*.

They are even more effective if they mention problems which were amicably resolved. We find that eight out of 10 companies overlook the benefit of reference letters or are reluctant to ask for them. They think reference letters are for used car salesmen only. But, what if they could honestly say to a prospect, 'I just had a letter in today from a client who had your same concern which we satisfied.' If you want to increase sales you have to be open minded to all ideas.

Why not develop a simple and unembarrassing way of asking for reference letters? Just ask the clients what they found beneficial or unique about your product or service and then ask if they would be kind enough to jot it down in their own words for us. Don't ask for the letter first. Ask for their opinion first. Then your job is easier.

Reference letters serve two purposes. First, they convince others of our reliability because a third party is more believable than our own stories.

Second, when people record their commendation in writing, it confirms it in their own mind. Therefore, they are more likely to remain customers and refer others than if they don't write. Memories are short, writing reinforces memories!

Quote facts and figures

Statistics give people a feeling of having a grip on solid facts. If you're using figures in writing, you'll want to note the difference between the written and the numerical form and the impact it makes on the reader. Which catches the eye first? Which gives a solid impression? You can write forty percent, 40% or 40 per cent. All give a different impression.

Try to quote the source, because the statistic has even more impact and credibility. 'In 1968 over 60% of the families in the USA owned their own home, *according to* Federal Reserve Board figures.' Because you are told the source, aren't you more likely to believe it? Most people are.

Quote satisfied customers

Quote satisfied customers, and be specific. 'Mr Smith in Pasadena used our machine 308 and he called to tell us that after three months his savings paid for the machine. He was really enthusiastic because it also saved him trips to the supplier which he estimated was worth four trips per week and four hours of his time.' Naturally you follow it with a question—'Would this kind of saving be a help to you?'

Use demonstrations

Nothing is more alive than the real thing. People buy with all their senses, not just their logical, analytical brain. A demonstration allows them to see and touch the product.

If you have two computer salespeople, one brings a video of the machine and proven statistics of its cost savings to the buyer, and the other brings the real thing. Who wins? Usually the demonstration because people love to touch and hold, to experiment, to do it themselves.

What if you're in the service industry? Think about all angles you can use. Recently I was doing a series of in-house seminars with the Lloyds Financial Futures people. On the first seminar, I had rejected the idea of demonstrations and didn't even suggest it to them, because I didn't see an angle.

But during the course they invited me down to the trading floor, and *voila*! I saw the visit as a perfect demo. The client could actually witness the service and see the benefits they would be getting.

Be inventive. Don't close your mind to these ideas. With a little ingenuity you can apply all these methods to your own business and increase your results.

Quote authorities

Quoting an authority or an expert in the field endorses a product. We buy it more readily. This has proven itself in advertising consumer items. And it works just as convincingly in large-scale industrial items. Many companies who are suppliers to British royalty are able to display a very prestigious symbol 'Supplier to Her Majesty the Queen'. They will testify to the endorsement it gives their product. What authority can you quote?

Use written material

The written word can be more convincing than the spoken word and appeals to peoples' visual senses. Literature, brochures and fact sheets all serve this purpose. It's important that the written copy be as neat and professional as possible. Generally the more upmarket the product, the more upmarket the brochure. All written material should state benefits as well as features. Charts, graphs, indented written format, all help to give it variety and reader appeal. So do photographs.

Use samples

Supplying a sample of the product gives customer appeal.

This is simple if the product is as small as a sugar cube. But what if it's bigger or more expensive?

What about a facsimile of the product? John Ryan at Heme International had a photographic replica made of the company's ammeter. It's small enough to fit in an envelope. The inside of the leaflet lists the benefits and features. The back suggests a demonstration and has a space for the agent's address details.

It also mentions the company's other products—current transducers. That's a lot of information to pack into an eight-inch by three-inch paper replica. The cut-out folded version is an irresistible 'touch me'.

Obviously a real sample is preferable. But if that's not possible, be inventive as John has, and save the sample for the demonstration.

Become skilled at nine methods

Use all of the nine alternatives for expressing our ideas in a way which influences decisions. By developing them now, isn't it easier to pull one out to use it, when you need it?

I'll never forget the plight of a management consultant I visited some time ago who had never had any sales training. He wanted to arrange a meeting with a large prospective client company. He called them and said simply 'John Jones is in town. We thought you might like to come over while he's here.' He didn't give any enticements. What impact would he have made using one of the nine illustrative methods—perhaps a verbal picture to motivate the buyer, perhaps a demonstration offer or a quote from a satisfied customer, perhaps sending literature or documentation ahead?

Next time you pick up the phone or go into a meeting, ask yourself what incentive you're offering the others for seeing things from your point of view.

The nine methods will help you. What closing ratio of convincing people do you have now? Why not measure your ability to convince others with each meeting or phone call, by using the nine methods? I promise you that your results will increase. I wouldn't bother telling you about them unless I'd seen them work in *all* industries.

Measure II—use a follow-up action system

Not only do we need to say the right thing, we have to say it at the right time. We need a system for follow up which is painless, which doesn't need thought to get started. It needs to be like a revolving wheel—once started, it carries you with it.

We've developed an internal system for sales follow-up which many of our clients have adopted. It's simple and so effective that we use a similar system for other office activities.

The system we've devised is a diary system. There are 52 pages in a notebook, one for each week.

Each page has five columns going down the page, one for each day. Down the page we put different headings such as 'call back' or 'send confirmation letter'. When we find out that Mr Jones is coming back on Friday, the 17th of March, we write 'Mr Jones, XYZ Co., 32a' in the 'call back' column of that week. Any other details about Mr Jones or the XYZ Company are kept in a file we've created called 32a. Then details don't clutter up the action sheet.

One of our management trainees, Josef Rutzel, even uses it in his personal life. When Josef went back to Wuerzburg, Germany, he scheduled his athletics, his hobbies, his friends and his thesis writing. He says that the system makes him twice as productive.

Rob Mann, of Lorient, and Sue Hume, who manages exports, use a system like this to monitor and control 'call in' inquiries. The company has always sent literature promptly. Now they can follow up systematically. The management controls which are created from a system like this bring peace of mind.

Measure III—display the results for everyone to see

The last step in the chain required to cure complacency is to publicize results. Not just sales results. Publicize everything. Tell how many calls were made. Tell how many calls resulted in conversation! Tell how many appointments were made. How many sales were made. How it compares to last week, last month.

Chart it, graph it, publicize it. Everybody needs to feel someone recognizes their achievement. They need to follow their own progress as well. Give it drama. Give it variety. Use bar graphs, line graphs and dot graphs.

Have you heard the story of the great steel tycoon who used to walk through the factory and mark a chalk number on the floor? Each shift finally realized the number referred to the previous shift's productivity. Soon they were marking their own chalk number and each was higher than the last. When we give people recognition, it inspires action.

Remember, to Stop Losing Business Needlessly:

**Take Preventative Medicine
Do the Right Thing, at the Right Time and
Display the Results.**

15

Personality Profiles— How To Work With Them

'No matter what I say, I don't seem to be able to get through. Why won't they decide to buy or not? They have all the facts, the best price, the fastest delivery – why won't they make a decision?' Does this sound familiar?

Frustrations like these are voiced daily by managers and sales people.

At Sykes Consultants, Bill and his people spend a great deal of time with clients in the assessment of personalities—the nature of people on the team as well as customers and clients. Why is this emphasis on people so important?

The answer is basic to human nature. Products and ideas are sold by people who build relationships with other people. The sales relationship is built upon values and needs just as any other relationship in life. The faster we learn to recognize those values and needs, the faster we will progress.

If we feel people understand us and we understand them, a relationship begins. Without understanding there can be fear and uncertainty and doors remain closed forever. If we can't 'read' the other person and they can't 'read' us then we will rarely sell successfully. Bill tells his clients that to succeed in understanding others we all have to be a mixture of amateur psychologists, sleuths, priests, and winners!

In our seminars to Develop Effective Sales, Bill and I alternate in leading the group through each segment of the course material. During the segment of Understanding Personality Profiles, Bill holds the attendees spellbound. Session after session regardless of who's attending, the personalities segment is one highlight of the seminar. One company director, Roger Whitlock, told us afterwards, 'If I had understood my co-director five years ago as I understand him after this session, we'd be light years ahead of where we are today.' He left the seminar with new insight and new methods of dealing with his partner's personality.

Why is it that this vital area of personalities is so little understood and so little studied? We spend years at school studying mathematics, reading and writing, but when it comes to personalities, the most vital of all aspects of life, we're left to our own devices.

How much we could do, as our seminar attendee, Roger, proved, if we took the time and effort to understand people and to understand the way our own personality affects others.

When two personalities come together in a room, it's a little like two chemicals coming together in a test tube. Each one affects the other. We wouldn't put two chemicals together in a test tube without knowing the properties of each! The reaction could be explosive.

Yet we often throw ourselves into situations with other people without knowing the 'properties' of each—the personality make-up of them, or of ourselves. No wonder the outcome is less than perfect.

If we took time to understand people, we could anticipate reactions and make changes before it's too late. We could add a buffer to lessen the impact in areas of difference. If you already do this, you're a rare individual indeed. Most don't. In fact, they do just the opposite.

Build trust through compatibility

Imagine the following scenario: a true story related by Bill at the seminars. Behind the desk sits a conservatively dressed buyer, with neat appearance, white shirt, dark suit and tie. The desk is clear with a white note pad, neatly headed with the meeting date and title, placed carefully on the middle of the desk.

The salesmen enters: bright red tie, and matching silk handkerchief showing flamboyantly from the pocket of his expensive suit, designer brief case, and a gold bracelet dangling at the cuff of the silk shirt. He offers a ready 'Good Morning'.

Did the two characters hit it off immediately? No, the salesman, not trained in responding differently to each personality type, failed to notice the hesitant reaction from the buyer. The desk chair moving further away, the reluctance to answer questions, the softening tone of his voice, were all clues to the buyer's personality.

What did the salesman do? He moved forward when the buyer withdrew, he asked more questions when the buyer hesitated. He raised his voice as the buyer lowered his. And so it went. The salesman responded in ways he knew best. The more aggressive he became, the more the buyer retreated.

Had he been a student of personalities, he would have known he needed to respond more like the other person to build compatibility. Without compatibility a relationship can't begin to grow. We need to show compatibility first. Later we can show our differences and strengthen our relationship. But first there needs to be common ground.

Statesmen do this when they negotiate on issues of worldwide importance. They start by getting a yes on issues of common ground, then they move to issues of diversity. Do you think they'd have any success if they started with the diversity? Not likely.

Everyone needs to feel there are compatible areas before they accept the differences. Shouldn't we all remember to respond in an acceptable way to our buyer the next time we're selling an idea or a product?

To be successful, we have to be adaptable. When dealing with conservative or analytical buyers, salespeople need to present the facts of the case and then back off, taking care to set times and dates for a follow-up call and religiously keeping to that appointment. This type of analytical, fact-finding buyer will resent any early intrusion into his world, unless it is at his invitation, and on his time and terms. A decision may never be made if compatibility is not fostered.

The successful salesperson will recognize these personality signals and treat each sales situation as a different campaign with a very different cast of characters. They will watch for the signs and signals from the prospect. They will adapt their style to build compatibility.

Learn from some, sell to others

One of Bill's closest colleagues, Norman Berry, practises this technique to perfection. For many years, Norman was Works Director of his family textile business in Yorkshire. With the decline of textiles and with the belief that hard work and integrity produce results, Norman started his own computer service bureau.

He had many early sales successes, but not enough to keep the home fire burning and the North of England cold out! He took on a line of security safes and was selling them over a large area.

On one sales call, he was faced with a husband and wife buying team, who owned a lock and safe store. The husband liked Norman and loved to talk. Norman discussed the business with him at first. He checked and cross checked the problems and the recent sales trends. Norman introduced a new price on his safes, discussed fast-moving lines, and so on.

A masterful display on Norman's part took place to understand the buying motives. Then Norman moved in for the sale.

At that point Norman turned to the wife and said, 'I understand you've already sold one floor safe this week, and had another inquiry yesterday. How about taking the three I have in the car. With the price reductions I've calculated, you should be able to sell those by the time I'm around next week.'

The sale was his. The order was signed by the wife. Norman knew that the husband was the one person not to sell to—conversations with him revealed buying motives, but when it came to getting the order, the wife was the person to see.

Many sales, and hours, have been lost by other salespeople who don't understand the personalities of the buying duo.

Opposite personalities complement each other. The same is true in corporations. If we *presume* that one person is the decision maker without looking deeper, we may be wasting our time.

We often need to do what Norman did—get our information from one, and sell to the other. Personalities complement each other and we need to direct our efforts properly to each. We need to learn from some and sell to others. We need to have the support of everyone.

Establish the key motivators, don't guess

Just as Norman knew, we must watch, listen and learn how to orchestrate the sale. It takes tenacity. It takes a desire to understand the other person and what makes them responsive.

Donald Moine, writing in *Psychology Today*, expressed the idea that sales, perhaps more than any other profession, is a psychological laboratory for testing human intelligence, persistence, persuasiveness and resilience, plus the ability to deal with rejection on a daily basis.

In the consulting field, Bill's company, Sykes Consultants, uses a personality profile predictor to screen and understand people's personal characteristics. As a qualified analyst, using this type of predictor, Bill is able to develop personality profiles of individuals who are likely to succeed in certain types of jobs. In sales and management jobs, it's particularly important to find out how certain types of people will interface with their own salespeople and with potential customers. The profiles also show how the personalities of individuals will interface.

As Roger from our seminar discovered, it's better to find out from testing rather than to spend a lifetime guessing. Sales managers, and indeed all company directors, need to recognize the styles and talents which are inherent in their successful salespeople. How else can they motivate their people to achieve the highest results?

Guessing at what motivates people can lead to disaster. Take salespeople for example. Studies consistently show there are many different motives which drive top salespeople to success. In Donald Moine's work on successful salespeople, several key motivators are identified. They include the need for status, control, respect, routine, accomplishment, stimulation and honesty.

Is that what you would have guessed about salespeople who achieve success?

Moine indicates that the best salespeople seek recognition as proof of their ability. They enjoy being with people and delight in influencing them. They need respect and want to be seen as experts on what is right, best or appropriate.

And, contrary to the common stereotype, most like routine and don't like having it interrupted. They need accomplishment, not just material comforts. After a while material rewards lose their ability to motivate.

They like to create new challenges such as going after 'impossible sales'. They make the impossible happen. They thrive on challenge and welcome outside stimulation to channel their high level of energy.

They have a strong need to believe in their product and service support. Their inner need for honesty means that they will switch jobs if the company reputation falls or the product quality declines.

These individual characteristics are only part of the story. One of the primary motivators in any sales team is the leader. The great industrialist Charles Schwab was noted for inspiring an amazing degree of co-operation in his people, as well as those with whom he had business dealings.

When Mr Schwab was asked what he considered the prime ingredient in his character that had helped make him such a success, he answered, 'I consider my ability to arouse enthusiasm among people the greatest asset I possess.' How many of us have learned to use undying enthusiasm in motivating ourselves and others? In order to do this we have to understand personalities.

People are still the greatest asset in marketing our products. We see many cultural differences between the nations of the world, and the problems these differences can cause in doing business. We need to establish people's motivation and it's not easy across cultures. We must make personal contact, and lots of it. We have to know others and let them know us. We have to sell ourselves before our products or services.

Bill and I see these differences at every turn. Regardless of business styles, one thing is universal. Marketeers must find common ground. And they must adapt to the buyer.

Understanding personality profiles, either through testing or simply by studying people's needs, is vital. If we are going to influence, coach and motivate our team into a dynamic sales force, or to sell our product and ideas, then we need to understand each and every person. For indeed, they are all different. They are all individuals with separate values and needs.

Let's join the superstars of sales who know that their selling style must be adapted to suit each individual buyer. It is up to the salesperson to do the adapting and not the buyer. Remember the buyer holds the order pad! Don't forget the red tie salesman who advanced as the buyer withdrew. Don't follow in his footsteps. If you want to succeed, take your cue from the successful.

Remember, to Stop Losing Business Needlessly:

**Recognize How Others are Motivated
and Develop a Common Ground for Trust**

Review of Part Five

Six Ways to
Stop
Losing Business Needlessly

Chapter 10   Why is 75% of All Business Lost on a Customer's First Contact with a Company?

1. Beware, Contact Points are Critical
2. Take Responsibility for Employee Performance
3. Attitudes. Some Need to be Changed
4. Concentration. The Human Factor

Chapter 11   Successful Interface Between Sales, Finance, Production and Service—Is It Essential?

1. Overcome Resistence to Selling
2. Improve the Relationship Between Departments

Chapter 12   The Lost Inquiry—More Common Than You Think

1. Treat Inquiries like Gold
2. Develop an Air Tight Tracking System
    Spot the Weaknesses
    Find the Cure
3. Put Every Lead into the System
    Track Exhibition and Advertising Leads
    Track Non Sales Department Leads
    Keep a Phone Log

Chapter 13   The Make or Break Buying Period

1. Don't Deny Your Customer Buying Cycle
2. Stop Fear and Improve Your Sales Methods
3. Improve Management Discipline and Motivation

Chapter 14   How to Cure Follow-Up Complacency

1. Take Preventative Measures
2. Increase Your Options for Putting Your Points Across
3. Use a Follow-Up Action System
4. Display the Results for Everyone to See

Chapter 15   Personality Profiles—How to Work with Them

1. Build Trust Through Compatibility
2. Learn from Some, Sell to Others
3. Establish the Key Motivation, Don't Guess

Part V Action Sheet

Ideas for Development:

- Make everyone responsible for sales
- Educate and motivate all departments to support sales
- Develop an airtight inquiry tracking system
- Close sales while the buying cycle is right
- Improve sales skills
- Develop an action system and display the results
-
-

Of the above ideas, which one is likely to yield the best results?

What percentage of sales (or performance) increase could realistically be expected?

How long would it take:
   to develop the idea?
   to get results?

Who would have to be involved?

What date should we start?

What is the first step I should take?

How To Analyse Your Current Situation And Develop Areas Of Improvement

16

Literature—Does it Sell or Tell?

What areas of literature could be updated to increase your sales return? One client of ours found out the hard way. His company was a foundry supplier and after 20 years of serving the UK, found its services were in demand overseas. Because it had never previously sold overseas, it had no need to put 'England' on its address—only the city and county.

One day after visiting the USA to generate business—a large investment for a company its size—the owner discovered he had missed out on a substantial bid, one he could easily have won, because his address was incomplete. The poor typist overseas simply typed the request for quotation exactly as he had it — city and county, no country. The envelope worked its way through the international mail network and landed on his desk a day after the closing date of the bid! A sadder director we have never seen.

The point is that many things about literature leave much to be desired. Not only are addresses incomplete—often features are unclear or unlisted and customers presume the product is less effective than the competitor's.

Literature is fundamental to all business activities. It is often the first contact that the customer has with the company. It represents the company, its products, its philosophy and its attitude to the customer.

Are you doing all you can to enhance this valuable way of communicating with your customer?

Are you making sure that your literature sells? If we expect to generate business, we have to tell our prospects how they can benefit by using our products. It's not enough just to list features. Features tell, they don't sell.

Develop a checklist

Let's look at some of the problems relating to literature, and ways of overcoming them quickly and cost effectively.

- Is the wording of our literature prepared by people with sales expertise who know how to state benefits clearly?
- Is the wording adequate for every level of decision maker, including technical, non-technical and financial managers?
- Does it include a clear and easy way to respond? Clear, full address including the country, if our work is international, clearly marked telephone number, department to be contacted, or better yet, an easy-to-use reply section such as a card, coupon or tear-off response slip, should be used.
- Do you have a big enough supply of literature to last past the next printing? If you run the risk of running short, you not only jeopardize sales, you also make your company look ineffective. People will ask, 'If they can't supply the literature, how can they supply the product?'

Reflect on the importance of stating features and benefits discussed in earlier chapters. Also, remember that the human mind is not capable of retaining information for long. People forget 80% of what they hear within two days. Therefore, literature should be used to jog the memory and to explain the benefits of your product in depth.

If your literature currently doesn't meet the above criteria, you are losing business needlessly.

You don't have to spend a vast sum of money or take a long time to rectify it. Here are some pointers:

For maximum effectiveness, if literature currently contains only technical information, in other words *features* without *benefits*, a separate sales sheet can be produced to supplement the technical literature.

A supplemental sheet to complement the current literature can be produced quickly and easily. A company we know which makes industrial machinery had a very technical, fact-filled piece of literature. It listed only features, no benefits. It therefore produced a single sheet which fitted inside its folded leaflet. It listed five main features in short bold headings, followed by the benefits in italic style print. It gave the address and telephone contact at the bottom with a ruled line around it which made it stand out very effectively.

Take corrective action quickly

This shows how quickly corrective action can be taken. The whole process was done on the word processor in less than a day with a very high quality look. The company then had a local quick print shop produce it on high sheen paper. It was cut, packaged and delivered to the company 48 hours later. The company's sales effectiveness was improved in less than three days at very little cost and energy.

Whether you want to produce a separate sales sheet such as this or redesign your literature all together remember: the purpose of literature is to let the customers know what the product is and how it will benefit them, thus enticing their interest, and refreshing their memories each time they read it.

- Be sure to state the benefits—how the customer will gain from using your product or service.
- Give proof and evidence of its quality and benefits, show referrals letters, news clippings, statistics. Give facts, quote experts, customers, and so on.
- Use enticement—give reasons which persuades customers to contact you now while their interest is high—limited time offers, samples offers, or an extra give away with the product.
- State your address and contact point clearly.

If you want to improve your returns take corrective action quickly on your literature. It can be fast, easy and cost effective.

Remember, to Develop Areas of Improvement:

Make Sure Your Literature Sells the Benefits as well as the Features

17

A 15-Point Checklist for Evaluating Sales Presentations

Mark McConnel was in his early 50s when appointed to take over the reins of a subsidiary of a publicly held service company. He had 15 years management experience with the company and before his appointment had been in charge of everything except sales and marketing. He knew the customers and the service inside out and seemed well qualified to head the company.

The first 18 months proved worrisome to the parent company and eventually to Mark. He knew sales were rocky under his new Sales Manager but he couldn't quite get a grip on it. The parent company could. They saw that Mark was leaving too much authority in the hands of the new man, without the controls, checks and balances which he used so successfully in running other facets of the company.

During these first 18 months there was a personnel turnover in sales of 52 people in an attempt to keep a steady team of 10.

No wonder Mark's ulcers flaired and the parent company grew cautious. But was it Mark's fault? Yes. Unfortunately, he just didn't know what to look for, what to believe or not to believe. If the Sales Manager and the Marketing Manager had two different stories, he had to go with one or the other on trust rather than experience and knowledge.

Mark realized, after coaching from HQ, that he needed to gain sales acumen. He needed to know the right questions to ask. He needed to know the difference between good and bad sales presentations so that he could judge the sales team's capability and not be putty in the hands of the Sales Manager. He also needed, as head of the company, to be able to give a decent sales presentation himself from time to time when the situation called for it, such as to banks and other financial institutions.

At first Mark was hesitant to get involved. He thought salesmen were born as salesmen and that he would never be one. He thought he should be able to leave sales in the hands of others who were hired for the job.

Finally, after a year and a half of chaos, the parent company gave Mark a do or die ultimatum. They insisted that he accompany their best sales personnel at HQ until he learned the tricks of the trade.

Mark was lucky. He survived the ordeal. They eventually removed the Sales Manager and put Mark in direct charge of the sales force for a period while he gained valuable hands-on experience. He learned that salesmen are made not born. He learned how to evaluate good and bad performance. He was lucky during those months of trial and tribulation that he had an already established customer base to rely on. Without that established customer base he would have been in a much more serious position. Others are not so lucky.

Many people running companies express uneasiness about having a grip on the sales side of their business. When it comes to product design, production or finance, they know where and how to lead the company. When it comes to sales, these directors are less confident. They feel there are too many unscientific parameters.

Often the same is true of owner operators. They need sales knowledge to lead their company into growth from day one. This is a key ingredient in getting a new company off the ground.

Realize that the whole is the sum of the parts

The checklist which follows was designed not only for people in Mark's position. It is also a vital reminder for all of us in sales and management who are committed to high performance from ourselves and our people.

Therefore, when using the checklist, remind yourself that you are looking at a series of ingredients. If you are going to perform at top efficiency, all the ingredients must be in place. If they are not, your performance sputters and spurts and sometimes comes to a complete halt. If you identify which ingredients need attention early enough, you can avoid coming to a standstill.

To use the checklist most effectively, consider:

- Which points meet high standards
- Which points need training or stronger control
- Ways you can support good performance as well as ways you can train and motivate in areas of weakness

Assess and improve each part

The checklist is used as a management control sheet. It allows quick and easy assessment of performance so that help can be given to each individual in the areas of current weakness. We all fluctuate on our strengths and weaknesses. The purpose of this monitoring is to stop current weaknesses and correct them swiftly so that the company can move ahead quickly. We want to increase the momentum of sales. This can only be done by having a constant eye on the fundamental of the business. Just as a hitch in the production process can ruin the product, so can a hitch in the sales process ruin sales momentum.

Remember, to Analyse Your Current Situation:

Use the 15-Point Checklist in Sales Presentations.

18

How to Recognize Sales Force Needs and Meet Them Cost Effectively

Jean Morgan-Bryant runs her own company in West London, and after only six years in business won one of the top awards for export achievement. As export merchants, Jean's peoples are on duty seven days a week, 52 weeks a year. They take calls for orders on Saturdays, at Christmas and during holidays, just like any other day. Their customers in the Middle East and Far East operate on different time zones and holidays, and want to find the Morgan-Bryant people at work available when they need them.

Obviously Jean's people have met the challenge of long hours, high performance and dedication to the job. Not many companies win the export award.

And obviously Jean has met the challenge of recognizing the needs of her sales force. What methods does she use to inspire this dedication and high performance?

Give personal attention to each need

Jean's answer is, 'Personal attention to everyone's needs.' Jean started with two people in 1979. In those days she did all the selling and all the customer liaison. By 1985 when they won the award, the company had a staff of 28. Jean had to 'transfer' her knowledge, her inspiration and her skill to all 28 people over that period.

'I used to sit at each sales desk, and show each person exactly how to handle customers.' She still does it on occasion, when the managers who now carry out that mentor role are away. 'People learn best and are motivated best by personal attention,' says Jean.

What about the time that this personal attention takes? Can it be cost effective? Jean believes emphatically that, 'If we train people properly, they can become a real resource.'

What did Jean have in mind about 'training people properly'. She gave me the following example. In the early days of the company she had a young man working for her who was bright, dedicated and good with customers.

He only had one weakness—numbers. 'Who doesn't have weaknesses,' thought Jean, 'We'll train him to use numbers better and he'll be a real asset to the company!' Sounds sensible? To Jean it did.

In most situations, people not as optimistic as Jean might have wondered. Numbers were an essential part of the business. Pricing, shipping, import duties—they all relied on numbers. Should Jean really spend her time with him, or should she look for someone with people skills and number skills?

No, attitude was more important to Jean than skill. Skill could be taught with the right patience and training. What was the outcome? The employee learned about numbers fast. His dedication remained. So did his skill with people. Jean was right, he did become 'a real asset to the company' as she predicted. His skills continued to increase and eventually he became a director of the company.

Everyone needs something different in order to become a top performer. Some need specific training as this young man did. Others need motivation, in ways as specific as this man needed training.

Skill areas which need attention are usually easy to spot. Motivational areas are not so easy. Often we think we know, but we find out later that we didn't.

What do you think is the biggest motivator for people? Most think it's a high salary.

I thought that was true until I read reports showing that pay ranked only third in people's order of priority.

The fundamental truth is that people are looking for something else besides pay as a motivator. You probably already know what it is. For most, as I've said before, but can't overstress, it's job satisfaction and recognition.

The point is, how many of us are operating under false pretences? How many of us are presuming we know what our employees want without asking?

Don't we stress the importance of finding out what the customers need before we decide which benefits to promote? Of course we do, otherwise we run the risk of promoting the wrong benefits and losing the sale.

Isn't the same true with employees? Shouldn't we find out their real wants and needs and provide those?

While writing this book, I met with the director of a major international conglomerate. Their subsidiaries range from shoe polish to oil field supplies. Their company had gone from strength to strength in recent years.

The man I spoke with worked for headquarters and interfaced with the subsidiaries. In talking with him about the skill and motivation of their people, I asked him what the secret was of their success. 'Our financial package is the biggest incentive,' he said.

But I wasn't satisfied. I asked what really motivated his people, what gave them their job satisfaction. Gradually we started to dig deeper into the management style of the company.

We started to see that the nucleus of the company was composed of people who had worked together closely for many years. That they had worked in teams to bring subsidiaries up from failure through to survival and finally growth. That their recognition of each other's capability extended into today's projects and that the challenge of bringing more companies into profitable positions far outweighed their financial compensation.

Learn the truth about recognition

So, there it was again, recognition and job satisfaction at the top of the sale of importance! But we ask ourselves, how do we recognize sales force needs? Aren't salespeople different from other employees?

The answer is yes. Salespeople are different. The difference is that they need even *more* recognition!

Why? The answer is quite basic and logical.

Take a minute to think about recognition. The opposite of recognition is rejection. Every day sales people are facing rejection. In fact, the proportion of rejection they face is higher than in any other job.

If they're doing their job right they face rejection day in and day out. They face it when trying to close a sale, when trying to make an appointment, and at every stage of objection throughout the sales process.

Rejection is a draining process. It drains us of our enthusiasm, our confidence, our zest in life.

Just as a battery which is drained needs recharging before it operates again, so do people.

Recognition is the charge we need to overcome rejection.

Usually those people who don't deal in sales, don't understand this. They find it annoying that salespeople require so much attention and recognition. Sometimes this annoyance leads to pulling back from giving the sales force what it really needs, and this causes their motivation to suffer.

As managers, we need to make people aware of sales force needs, if we are to get the best results. We need everyone pulling together.

The next time you ponder over ways to motivate the sales force, you can focus on ways to restore recognition, ways to recharge the battery. The results are immediate, as well as cost effective.

Recognition comes in many forms. It comes in listening to people— listening to their ideas, their problems, their goals, their needs. One-to-one communication can be the most powerful motivator in the world.

Do you realize how much the employee gains from the attention of the boss? A once a week, undivided half hour of face-to-face contact with the immediate boss does more for motivation than five dozen quick hellos.

In big companies, 15 minutes with the Chief Executive will carry an employee through the year, or even through his career.

If you doubt that, you haven't met a good Chief Executive. The exceptional ones I know give recognition to the employee for his or her specific performance. They relate it to the company's success as easily and sincerely as anything in life.

They've learned that a person's continued motivation is reliant upon the recognition of their efforts and contribution. Shouldn't we all take time to develop the same skill and understanding?

Is this kind of recognition expensive? No.

Recognition comes in many forms and all bring cost-effective results. It can be seeing one's name in print, a written or verbal announcement of competition winners, target achievers, and so on.

It can be verbal recognition to an individual or a group at a management meeting, a committee meeting or a council meeting.

One of the best group motivators I've ever met is Keith Barrett who chaired the executive committee of the London Chamber of Commerce and Industry West Section during the committee's first years of existence, before I became Chairman. It was always a pleasure to work with the committee because of Keith's exceptional ability to give positive reinforcement and recognition to the group for its actions.

His recognition was always to the point. Statements such as 'Due to your enormous support and hard work, we've now achieved such and such,' or 'As everyone in this room knows . . .' kept each of us involved and working toward the committee's goals.

There's no doubt in my mind that in Keith's role as Personnel Director of Glaxo Pharmaceuticals, he keeps contributions from those in the company equally as high.

Shouldn't we all use specific recognition to ensure the highest contribution from our people? Shouldn't we take the advice of Jean Morgan-Bryant who won the export award, and give personal attention to everyone's needs?

What does each person in your team need? Each is different, and spending time with them is essential if we are to recognize their needs and motivate them to the highest possible performance.

Remember, to Develop Area of Improvement:

Recharge the motivational battery with recognition.

19

What Business are We Really In?

If the railroad barons in the United States had sat down 50 years ago and defined the business they were really in, the nature of their companies would be completely different. Their real business, of course, was not the railroads itself, but transportation.

When air transportation arrived, they should have had the foresight to get involved in it, and not be left behind. They would have prevented their dramatic decline in sales.

Believe it or not, business, and even governments, often see their role differently from how their customers see it. We have all seen government five-year plans which have been scrapped at the end of the first or second year. We have seen businesses with annual budgets set in January which rapidly change into operating budget number one by March and operating budget two by June due to sales and expenditure not meeting their plan.

This level of uncertainty or irrelevant planning can be caused by an inadequate definition of the customers with which we are really trading. Do we really understand why our customers are dealing with us? Have we identified why we are unique and what single special advantage we do have over our competition?

Don't use yesterday as tomorrow's guideline

Many managers assume they know what their business really is because they inherited a successful product line with apparent growth and an improving market share. It is often the case that products with an improving or commanding lead in competitiveness are the very ones which have already become obsolete. The embryonic new mode of transport, the aeroplane, was created long before it was realized that the railroads were a declining business.

Peter Drucker[1] warns everyone in his book *The Practice of Manage-*

ment to be sure we know what our business really is. This is almost always a difficult question. Drucker feels that can be answered only after hard thinking and studying. The right answer is usually anything but obvious.

Find new applications

Take the business definition for a firm such as Church and Dwight Company. It produces 'Pure Baking Soda' under the brand name of Arm and Hammer. The answer to its question—'What business are we in?'—is indeed anything but obvious.

Church and Dwight has for 135 years represented the 'standard of purity and quality', as its packaging states, for one of its products, the most common and ordinary one—pure bicarbonate of soda. However, the management team has used an enlightened approach to redefine and broaden the business areas in which pure bicarbonate of soda competes. Not once, not twice, but at least five times!

In addition to its product acting as a leavening agent for the food industry when mixed with cream of tartar, it is also used medically for heartburn and the prevention of plaque on teeth. Still further afield is its use as a cleaning agent, a mild abrasive for the refrigerator, and yet again as a substance for absorbing food odours.

Can you think of anything broader than these five applications for the same product? One is for human consumption, two applications are medical, two are cleaning related. Yet for all five it is identically the same product. Can you diversify your application area? You may be surprised and your discovery can lead to new profits from new markets.

Sykes Consultants had a client with a similar opportunity. But the opportunity, like Arm and Hammer's, had to be discovered.

The company was faced with a product in the textile industry which was sadly and rapidly declining. It was being overtaken by man-made materials and inevitably cheaper imports. However, the fine natural qualities of the original product still attracted a loyal following, particularly with users who had to comply with the new, stringent fire regulations.

This application wasn't obvious to those who didn't look. A potentially huge new market has opened up for this company utilizing its existing manufacturing technology and channels of distribution. The competition are apparently unaware of this application. Their mind is still buried in yesterday's business.

This is a classic example of never accepting the obvious, never writing off the most basic of products. Ask yourself what consumers want that they haven't got. It is the ability to ask this question and to answer it correctly that usually makes the difference between a growth company and one that depends on the rising tide of the economy or industry for its development. Take the lead when looking for new applications for your product. Increase sales on your own merit, not on chance.

Utilize the same distribution channels

How far afield should we go with applications? How quickly should we move?

Peters and Waterman suggest, in *In Search of Excellence*[2], that excellent companies stick to what they are best at and only move one manageable step at a time.

These companies kept to the business they knew best and when entering new fields, they did it carefully. The best companies did not jump in too quickly. They tested the waters carefully first and if they didn't have success, they quickly withdrew.

When we are challenging the nature of the business we are in, we should be careful that we are not too radical in moving into totally uncharted waters. In the case of the Arm and Hammer product, the company's same channels of distribution were used, thus lessening the risk of moving into unchartered ground.

When we're looking for areas of improvement, we have to keep our eye on the customer. Where are they going with their needs? Remember the railroads. Remember the customers wanted transport, but not necessarily train transport. Focus on the fact that, with ingenuity, you can find new application areas for your products and services.

[1] Peter Drucker. The Practice of Management (London: Mercury Books, Weinemann Group, 1965), pp. 46, 54.

[2] Thomas Peters and Robert Waterman, Jr., In Search of Excellence (New York, Warner Books, 1984).

Remember, to Develop Areas of Improvement:

Always look ahead for where your customers are going and for new application area for your current product.

20

What Separates Sales from Marketing?

I find it absolutely fascinating that there is so much controversy over the difference between sales and marketing.

Invariably at the start of our sales seminars someone takes Bill or me aside and says, 'I must get this issue cleared up. I'm embarrassed to ask, but what is the *real* difference between sales and marketing?'

It's like asking the difference between a course and a seminar. We don't really care what it's called, do we, as long as we get results from it. What we do want is to make sure that the *content is right* and that the *person running it is right*.

It's the same way with sales and marketing. First, you want to make sure that the content is right. Do you have everything in it that you need for your company? Your company needs:

- Change as your company grows, as your product line changes and so on.
- Change as your customer base changes—when you start selling to a different industry, a different country, a different customer group.

Second, we want to make sure that the person running it is right. Do they have the skills they need to handle the content? If you go to a seminar called the 'Basics of Flying' you don't want to find out its being run by Henry Kissinger, unless Henry is a pilot. You might like to hear Henry talk about politics, but for your purpose at that moment, you want to hear an expert on flying.

It's the same in sales and marketing. You don't want a person who is good at marketing running sales or vice versa. There are many component parts in each.

All these require different skills. The skills of your people are different as they themselves develop *and* as your personnel changes.

The important thing is to make sure that every part of the job is being carried out properly by people best able to handle that function. What fits your organization today, may not be right tomorrow.

We live in a fast-changing world. We often find people being a slave to a structure which fitted the organization and its people last year but not this year. All parts of the job must be carried out for a company to be successful, whether it falls under the marketing banner or the sales banner.

Adopt a flexible approach

The companies with the best results take a flexible approach to the sales and marketing functions. As with work allocations on any project, organizational changes must be made to match the company's people resources.

IBM for example undertakes organizational changes as a matter of course. In some divisions it's rare for three to six months to pass without a major reshuffle in work load allocation. This happens normally as staff capability and company needs change.

The same is true of sales and marketing. It may seem logical to put a certain function under the heading of sales or the heading of marketing. But if the staff available are not equipped to handle one function and can handle another function better, then a reshuffle is necessary.

If you want to move fast and improve returns, you have to look for the best people to handle the functions and be prepared to be flexible. You may run into resistance from people when a change is being contemplated, but that's one of the important roles of managers—the ability to handle objections and sell ideas in such a way that the employees see benefits for themselves and the company.

If your functions are not handled by the best people for the job, then you're not getting the best results. If you need to inspire change, you'll have to sell your ideas. As we said in earlier chapters, give them the facts and the benefits to let them 'buy' your ideas. As every motivator knows, you are sure to get results when people support your ideas. To force issues without support is certain death. Even the best idea is sure to be undermined one way or another if you haven't 'sold' the idea in terms of the benefits which other people will gain.

Make sure all functions are carried out by the best qualified people

Regardless of how a company decides to allocate its sales and marketing functions, certain key resposibilities should be considered. Usually the responsibility for the functions are allocated as in Figure 4.

Within each function, the variety of tasks handled will vary according to each company's needs. The important thing in achieving high results is to be sure that good, solid, airtight tracking systems are in place and that someone is held responsible for each function. Grey areas create chaos and chaos rarely brings results. Tracking systems will ensure that no enquiries are lost and that all sales practices are carried out on time.

Pick the hierarchy that suits your needs

An area of intense interest to companies is the hierarchy of the sales and marketing command. Should the sales side report to the marketing or vice versa? Or should they both report to the company or division head?

In companies where personalities, skills or views clash between sales and marketing, not an uncommon occurrence, the most workable

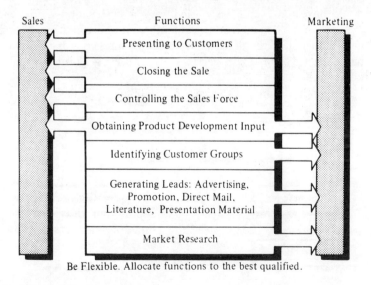

Be Flexible. Allocate functions to the best qualified.

Figure 4   The allocation of functions

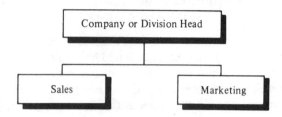

Figure 5   The sales and marketing hierarchy

solution is the one shown in Figure 5. This can actually be healthy because strong ideas with different perspectives will go straight to the top for filtering.

The issue of whether sales should report to marketing or marketing to sales is determined by company preference (Figure 6).

While the approach on the left of the figure is more traditional, we're finding that more large companies, especially in Europe, are moving toward the approach on the right. Their argument is that the marketing function provides more perspective, is more analytical by nature and should have the overall responsibility. Our observation is that the decision is not based on rationale but rather on who is at the top. More often than not, if the decision maker has a marketing background, marketing will reign. If sales, sales will reign. So let's get away from party politics and on to results.

The important thing is to have, 'The right people in the right place,

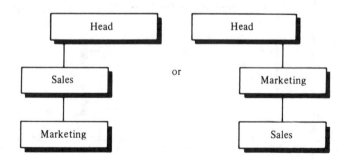

Figure 6   The marketing–sales or sales–marketing hierarchy

at the right time.' There are two ingredients to success.

- *Whoever reigns must understand both functions.*
- *Whoever reigns must be a good motivator.*

Without these two ingredients, you will fail.

Change functional responsibility as your needs change

The next issue of interest, particularly with small and growing companies, is the question of adding sales and marketing people for the first time. How and when do we delegate these responsibilities away from the company head and bring in a new person? Should it be a sales function or a marketing function? The growth development in small companies usually looks like that shown in Figure 7.

In this initial stage company heads usually handle sales and marketing functions themselves along with other responsibilities.

Although they may not feel they are large enough to treat sales and marketing as special functions, they are nevertheless producing literature, selling the products or service, planning product development and so on.

Company Head Includes
Sales and Marketing
in Own Responsibilities

Figure 7   Stage 1: company heads handling sales and marketing functions

The next stage is to bring in one additional staff member to take part of the load off the company head. Usually we find that the new person handles sales while the company head continues with marketing decisions related to advertising, promotion, exhibitions and so on. But it doesn't have to be that way. The company head could hand over the marketing task and keep the sales (Figure 8).

Figure 8   Stage 2: company heads delegating the sales function but retaining the marketing function

Later the company head may feel he or she needs to delegate more responsibility and may pass marketing over also (Figure 9).

With the right management controls in place, these moves usually stimulate growth, because it allows the company head to have more time for planning and management.

Also, since they have controlled the function themselves, they can quickly pinpoint areas of the job which are being handled well or need improvement. Therefore the changeover of responsibility is usually less dramatic and more effective than people anticipate. Many small companies delay this delegation step for fear of disruption and yet, when finally taking the leap, say that it was the most important step in their development.

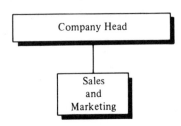

Figure 9   Stage 3: company heads delegating the sales and marketing functions

When we think about this dilemma, we see that the situation for small companies is no different than it is for large companies. It's a matter of being flexible—it's recognizing the changing needs of the company and the capability of the people available.

A person who is too stretched for time is no different from a person without capability—the job won't get done effectively either way. Good managers have learned that surrounding themselves with good people brings rapid results, whether they run large or small companies.

Remember, to Develop Areas of Improvement:

Put people in charge of functions according to their ability and the changing needs of the organization.

21

Management Controls—How to Make Them Effective

When my husband and I first took our boat out into the English Channel, the first thing we encountered near the coastline was a series of buoys floating in the water. These buoys stood up out of the water a few feet and had flashing coloured lights on them.

Each buoy had different colours and we had to check the colours flashing on each one, then check our navigational chart which showed which colour lights we should pass to be sure we were going in the direction we intended to go.

It sounds easy, but it wasn't. The buoys were coming up fast, so by the time we checked the buoy on the right and the one on the left against the chart we were on the next set of buoys. The shoreline was getting further and further away and the feeling of being in 'deep water' was literal.

We could see how easy it would be to go off course. If we didn't take corrective action immediately, we would be in big trouble. After two or three sets of wrong buoys, we knew it would be very difficult to get back on course. The weather could change and the current could be against us.

After passing three wrong buoys, getting on course again is more difficult than after one wrong buoy.

We don't go out to sea without charting our way ahead, and we don't set off and leave the chart behind. Because of the hazards at sea, we know every step of the way, whether we are on course or not. And when we go off course the first time, all hands are at the helm to help us back on course.

So it should be with management controls. It links actual performance to the plan. Isn't the direction we're going in business as important as the direction we're going at sea? Isn't it just as difficult to get back on course once we're off, as it is at sea? Many companies think that they can record results and only compare it to their plan every three months, or every year, or worse yet, never. 'We'll see where we'll go when we get out there.' A bit hazardous in the deep sea.

In business, just as at sea, we have currents which work against us. The farther we let ourselves drift off course, the harder it will be to get back on when the currents come along. What if we don't take our plan with us?

If You Don't Know Where You're Going, You'll Probably End Up Somewhere Else. That's the light-hearted title for the thought-provoking book written in the 1970s by Dr David Campbell.[1] His inherent message is timeless. If we don't have our plan with us to guide us every step of the way, we'll end up someplace else. That's expensive for business. And it's frustrating in life. We must have controls in business.

The best control is the ability to check actual sales performance against the plan on a regular, short interval basis. Then, like the captain at sea, you can take quick corrective action when you start to go off course.

If the intervals are too long between checking performance against the plan, it's more difficult to get back on course.

If this necessity for checking performance against the plan to have control is so self evident, why aren't companies using management controls to get better results?

Don't mistake reporting systems for control

The first reason is that they sometimes mistake a reporting system for management control. A management control system must link actual performance to the plan.

A system which records only the past performance without linking it to the company plans is *not a control system*. It's *only a reporting system*.

This is more common than you think. Bill and I have known company directors, both in our consulting and in the seminars, who say, 'We have great management controls. We have performance reports coming off our computer as often as we want them. Yes, we have more than enough controls.'

What they don't realize is that reports are not controls. What good does it do you to know where you are if you don't know where you should be?

---

[1] David Campbell, Ph.D., *If You Don't Know Where You're Going, You'll Probably End Up Somewhere Else* (Niles, IL: Angus Communications, 1974).

Therefore, controls aren't as good as they could be because the results aren't compared against the plan often enough. Then we also have to consider the plan itself.

When you're examining your plan, the question you need to ask yourself is, 'Do we have our plan broken down into meaningful segments?' Each segment will serve as a guidepost, like the buoys in the sea, to give you a clear, concise indication of where you are. If the segments are derived accurately, they help you plan where you want to go.

The segmentation can be very useful in looking at each product group. If you look at the sales figures within product groups objectively, you see things which help you with your plan.

Use your history to segment your plan

Usually you need to know something about your past in order to look at the future objectively.

If you're going to build an effective growth strategy, you need to know where your strengths have been and look for a trend for the future. You need to know *exactly* which product sectors you've had the most success in. You need to know *exactly* which customer sectors have been most important.

Your plan will only be as good as your precise knowledge of your company. I say precise because all of us have impressions of the past which prove to be less than accurate when we look closely at actual data.

We might have a lasting impression of an agent who performed well two year ago and, regardless of his recent performance, we might still be clinging optimistically to that market long after hope is gone.

We might have a lasting impression of three big orders in one product category and lose sight of the fact that the small orders together are more important.

In order to be objective, we have to see actual facts, not just rely on hearsay, or on memory of past sales.

If you don't see your situation accurately, your plan won't serve you as well as it could.

You might think that your gut feeling is right about sales breakdown by product and by customer or by territory but until you get it down on paper, in black and white, it's meaningless.

Chart your history

I advocate getting statistics on sales breakdowns into chart form. A picture is worth a thousand words.

Here's what happened to a machinery company we worked with. They had figures which remained static for almost a five-year period. But the sales figures remained static only because of inflation. The actual number of products they were selling each year was going down. They quickly bundled together the numbers of units sold for each

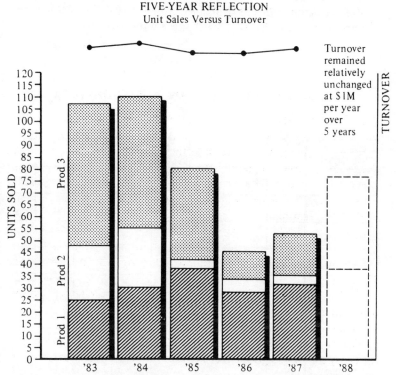

FIVE-YEAR REFLECTION
Unit Sales Versus Turnover

The bar graph shows quickly that product group 2 is looking hopeless, group 1 is holding its own, and group 3 is making a comeback. By looking at the number of units sold, rather than just the turnover, you now have accurate, indisputable facts about each product segment. You can see the trends. You can combine these trends with your knowledge of market demands to determine the plan for the future.

Figure 10   Charting your history

product group, and put the unit figures in bar graph form. This gave the directors a new perspective (Figure 10).

You can use segmentation not only to understand product group as the company above did, but also to understand each customer group.

Gerry Lancaster and Malcolm Breeze did this successfully. They run Kort Propulsion, a very prestigious company in the marine engineering industry. They design nozzles for ship propellers which improve fuel efficiency, velocity and manoeuvrability. The nozzles are fitted to everything from naval ships and tugs to small fishing boats.

Gerry and Malcolm decided that their sales history should be broken into finer detail than was available on their day-to-day management report in order to develop a plan for the future.

PAST SALES ANALYSIS HELPS YOU PLAN THE FUTURE
By Industry, By Area

	Naval	Tug	Oil Rig Supply Vessel	Fishing	Drilling	Bulk Carrier	Ferries	Workboat
USA Sector A	★★★★★★★★	★★★★★★		★★★★★★★★★★★★★★★★★★★★★★	★	★★★		
USA Sector B		★★★★★★★		★★★★★★★★★★★★★★★★★★★★				★★★★★★★★★★★★
USA Sector C		★★		★★★★★★★★★★★★★★★★★★★★				
UK		★★		★★★	★			
Canada				★★★★★				
Egypt		★					★★★★★★★	
Norway		★★★	★★★	★	★			
Iceland								
Singapore		★★★★	★★★					
Holland		★★	★					

(This example has had the statistics and countries altered, so as to protect the company's confidentiality.)

Figure 11   Past sales analysis helps you plan the future

Malcolm divided his sales statistics into product sectors and then into territory sectors. He put it into an easily digestible graph. One look at the graph gave him more insight than written figures.

He could easily see that the fishing sector produced a high volume of orders.

He was now in a position to ask himself questions about where to take his company in the future.

The fishing sector produced more unit sales but the naval sector produced higher value sales.

What if Malcolm hadn't produced the graph, but only saw the sales figures on paper? He, like most companies, would only know the total sales value. He wouldn't know how many units were sold to shipping and naval. He wouldn't know which countries each were sold to.

Segmenting your products sold by industry allows you to see at a glance exactly what's happening. It's detailed. It's specific, not general. When you work with specifics, you can plan for specific results. When you work with generalities, you can only plan results in generalities.

Make your plan, then compare your results daily

Doesn't segmenting make sense? Use it for planning the future after you've analysed the past.

In our Develop Effective Sales seminars, Bill and I have members focus on specific areas of past performance, then plan the future.

By doing this, they can accurately see their strengths and know more about what customers have really wanted from them. Only then can they plan their future. And, only by having a segmented plan, can they have management controls.

Here's an example:

One seminar attendee, Bob Williams, had a plan for a 20% growth for his company in the next year. We encouraged him to divide his growth targets into specific segments.

So he said, 'OK, we'll increase our sales to our current customers by 10%, and get the other 10% from completely new customers.'

'And when will your reps have time to visit the new prospects?'

'Oh, they'll just fit that in', he said.

'Well, let's see,' we said. 'Let's just see how many appointments they need to do. And don't forget the calls to make the appointments as well. Let's do a little analysis, and see how much work it amounts to for each rep each day. Then, when you know *exactly* what's required you can *monitor* and *control* it.'

We were going gently with Bob, but we know that if he didn't have an exact plan, he wouldn't know when he was going off course. If he didn't know exactly what activity was needed day by day, by each person, he wouldn't know if his growth was on target. He would be letting it go to chance until the end of the month or the end of the year.

'OK, Bob, let's start from the top. We'll flip chart it'. It looked like this:

Growth plan
segmented for management control purposes

Goal: 20% growth wanted.
How: 10% from new, 10% from old customers.

Breakdown of total workload:

Business from new customers

10% growth will mean we need 100 new customers.
We will have to see 10 prospects in order to gain one new customer.
Therefore 1,000 prospects need to be seen.
Each prospect will need approximately five telephone calls before an appointment can be arranged.
Therefore 5,000 phone calls need to be made. (Add here any other workload requirements such as mailshots or direct mail to be sent, etc.)

Business from old customers

10% growth will mean we need new business from 100 old customers.
We will have to see three old customers in order to gain business from one.
Therefore 300 old customers need to be seen.
Each old customer will need approximately two telephone calls before an appointment can be arranged.
Therefore 600 phone calls need to be made.

Total:
1,300 customers need to be seen (1,000 new and 300 old).
5,600 phone calls need to be made to make appointments (5,000 to new and 600 to old customers).

Breakdown of daily workload for growth:

Time allocation.

Let's say we have 50 weeks (52 minus two for holidays, etc.).

This breaks down to 20 new prospects each week (1000÷50 weeks).

And six old customers each week (300÷50 weeks).

We have five days per week.

Therefore five to six prospects and old clients need to be seen each day (26 divided by five days).

This breaks down to four prospects each day (20 divided by five days), and one to two old customers each day (six divided by five days).

Divide this by the number of sales people you have, and you have the true daily workload for appointments.

But we're not finished yet. Repeat the process for the number of telephone calls which need to be made daily, per person.

If the results astound you, look again. You may want to reallocate work to other members of staff or create other solutions. It's better to find out now, then monitor and control it throughout the year, than to ignore the workload and find out too late that your targets are not going to be met.

This same system works for small companies. A woman I know wanted to start a chain of distributors to sell health products. Her plan was to distribute leaflets to entice would-be distributors to come for evening demonstrations. She asked my advice on the plan and I had her do the above analysis.

She quickly saw the number of distributors she wanted would require many times more leaflets and evening demonstrations than were possible. So, she changed her strategy to include advertising and other methods. But without doing the analysis, she told me she would have wasted six months of effort. Her failure would have been in not stopping to analyse how many people would need to be seen to convert one to an actual distributor, then, to go further and analyse how many leaflets were required to get that many people into a room for a demonstration.

This is a typical shortcoming of small companies and large, so don't be complacent. Have a *daily* monitor and control system.

If your people need to make 10 telephone calls per day to make prospect appointments, make sure it's done.

If they don't make 10 calls on Monday, they'll have 20 on Tuesday. If they skip Monday and Tuesday, they have 30 to make on Wednesday.

You see the problem. Most people try to 'fit it in'. They work *without* a monitor and control system.

On the above basis, if you let your new customer acquisition go until the end of the month, you'll have 200 phone calls to do. That's why most sales targets are lost. People don't segment them into daily tasks.

Use specifics in developing your plan and in measuring the results against the plan each step of the way. Keep your plan with you and compare your results to the plan every step of the way.

Remember, to Develop Areas of Improvement:

**Segment your plan and your results,
then compare, compare, compare.**

Review of Part Six

How to Analyse Your Current Situation and Develop Areas of Improvement

Chapter 16 Literature—Does it Sell or Tell?

1. Develop a Check List
2. Take Corrective Action Quickly

Chapter 17 A 15-Point Check List for Evaluating Sales Presentations

1. Realize that the whole is the sum of the parts
2. Assess and Improve each part

Chapter 18 Recognize Sales Force Needs and Meet Them Cost Effectively

1. Give Personal Attention to Each Need
2. Learn the Truth about Recognition

Chapter 19 What Business are We Really In?

1. Don't Use Yesterday As Tomorrow's Guideline
2. Find New Application Areas
3. Utilize the Same Distribution Channels

Chapter 20   What Separates Sales from Marketing?

1. Adopt a Flexible Approach
2. Make Sure all Functions are Carried Out by the Best Qualified People
3. Change Functional Responsibility as Your Needs Change

Chapter 21   Management Controls—How to Make Them Effective

1. Don't Mistake Reporting Systems for Control
2. Use Your History to Segment Your Plan
3. Chart Your History
4. Make Your Plan, Then Compare Your Results *Daily*

Part VI Action Sheet

Ideas for Development:

- Make sure literature sells the benefits, not just the features
- Become proficient at all 15 points of effective sales presentations
- Recharge motivation through recognition
- Look ahead and find new application areas
- Assign people to functions according to ability, not tradition. Recognize the changing needs of the organization
- Segment our plan and our results into workable short-term units. Then compare regularly
-
-

Of the above ideas, which one is likely to yield the best results?

What percentage of sales (or performance) increase could realistically be expected?

How long would it take:
    to develop the idea?
    to get results?

Who would have to be involved?

What date should we start?

What is the first step I should take?

Successes And Failures In Overseas Markets

22

How to Plan Your Entry for Maximum Results

Yes, sales into foreign markets can be extremely lucrative. The Japanese have been teaching the world that lesson for some time. Some companies in the eastern and western world sell exclusively to export markets. If they can sell all of their goods abroad, it stands to reason that most of us can sell some of our goods abroad.

The question is—how to enter as profitably as possible, with as few mistakes as possible. And competition is growing. In 1985, I attended a conference addressed by Charles Price, the US Ambassador to Britain. It was indicated that five American companies account for 11% of the total American export revenue. Only 30,000 American companies look abroad for business.

There's no time to waste. Competition is increasing. If we don't learn to meet the competitors head on in overseas markets, we'll be facing them in our own markets.

Two companies were recently portrayed on television. Both made the same product. One had outdated production and management techniques. They were losing ground rapidly to the Korean imports. The other company had developed high productivity by investing in machinery and by putting management controls and incentives into place. They were selling successfully against the Koreans on the Korean's home ground—with identically the same product!

The first company complained that 'Our problem is lack of government intervention. We want protection against imports.' The second company knew that reliance on government policy was speculative. They took *responsibility for their own future* and planned a success strategy that would work—with or without government intervention.

Regardless of what we believe about protection from imports, the fact is that we cannot predict government policy. If we are to profit, we have to develop our own ways to succeed.

Whether we export or not, we need to understand foreign products and marketing. We'll be faced with these, here and abroad. The sooner we grasp the differences, the sooner we succeed.

Getting into foreign markets profitably is a three-step process. One is the plan, two is the implementation, three is the follow-up. Where many companies go wrong is with the plan, then the implementation and follow-up are worthless. It becomes an exercise of throwing good money after bad.

The answer is to look at all the alternatives. Then you can decide which is most lucrative as part of your planning process.

First, plan carefully considering all options

One company came to us and specified that they wanted us to find and appoint distributors for them in overseas market. They had already rejected setting up their own premises. They thought that direct sales through distributors was the only alternative. But we thought that direct export did not look promising because the exchange rate had turned against them.

After investigating the market, we were attracted to another option. What if they were to manufacture under licence? By licensing they could sell their technology and in return get a front end fee and royalties. They stood to gain more that way than they would by direct sales.

They would have three benefits. First, they would have a yearly income from royalties with an agreed minimum guarantee. Second, they would have less management and staff involvement, meaning that they could use their time for other expansion activities. And third, they would not have to finance any expansion of their manufacturing facility. That is certainly a lucrative alternative to consider.

Look at your alternatives in depth. Don't have blinker vision, don't restrict your opportunities to what works in other places. A foreign market is indeed foreign. The culture is different and so are the opportunities.

When you're planning your market entry, be sure to look at all alternatives.

It takes a little more time and a little more ingenuity, but the results pay off.

The opportunity to 'licence' to sell was often thought of as relating to developing countries. But that's not the case. It works well between or within any set of countries because the buyers may find it cheaper to purchase your expertise than to develop their own. For you, the seller, a know-how fee plus on-going royalties may prove to be more profitable than selling the product direct.

A large investment bank we worked with wanted to fund a textile factory which would product $13,000,000 worth of clothing each year. They could have drawn upon local expertise to set up the factory and the product line, but they didn't.

They knew from previous experience that buying in the know-how for the production and product line would save time. Because of buying in the technology, several of their previous factory start-ups showed profits within one year of incorporation. We worked with them to find a licensor.

The point is, you need to choose the method which is right for you. Don't go for convenience. Cutting the plan short will lead to disaster in the implementation and follow-up stages. You'll spend time and money trying to make something out of nothing.

A common error companies make is to appoint agents they meet at an exhibition stand. They may seem right at the time, but further investigation later proves they don't have the right sales contacts, service capability and so on. A trip to the country saves you throwing good money after bad.

What's right for your competitors or right for you five years from now, may not be right today. When it comes to acquisitions, joint ventures and setting up premises, you need to proceed with caution. Be sure you know the culture and the marketplace.

Bill tells the story of two different companies—one company American and one British—trying to get into each other's markets.

The British company bought out an American company and *afterwards* discovered that the salaries of the American staff were much higher than of the British counterparts. So they reduced the salaries of the American executives, and then wondered why they weren't content to stay! They thought the Americans would stay because the bigger parent company would offer more career opportunities. They were wrong. They found themselves trying to run a new company in a country they knew nothing about, with no experienced executives.

In the other story, an American company, new to foreign marketing, did this. The company decided they would set up premises in Europe. They would have one location in England to serve Norway, France, Sweden and England with no local support in the other three countries. Their idea that they could sell direct, without agents and without people who spoke the language and knew the culture, brought them disastrous results. Had they examined their options, such as appointing local agents and distributors they would have achieved better results. Although both companies did well in their own market, they failed to choose the right options when their company entered overseas markets.

Options like licensing look complicated to some companies on the surface, but when they dig deeper into it, they see it is less complicated than taking an 'obvious' route like the two companies above. All options should be considered, if you want to maximize your success.

Don't take what looks like an easy route and then find out, half way down the road, that it's the wrong choice.

Second, implement the plan going around the road blocks

When you're getting into a market, put your best foot forward. Present yourself properly.

Don't send the wrong person or the wrong literature. Don't go unprepared. Believe it or not, we've seen heads of companies go abroad with no literature, no photographs, no samples! They're too pressed for time and so unprepared that they throw away their opportunity.

If you don't know the market, don't try to make decisions without local expertise. Dealing in foreign markets is like working your way through a maze in the shortest possible time. To get guidance through the maze, you would chose an expert to show you through — someone with proven ability, not a man on the street that's never been through it before.

At the implementation stage, you'll find obstacles. You need people who can overcome the obstacles.

We had a client company in textile supplies wanting to sell into a third world country. But its product was on the restricted list. So it thought it would have to set up a local operation to either produce or package the product there. But our consultant, who knew the governmental decision-making process, had other ideas. He was able to link the company up with a local manufacturer who *could* import the product because he had the authority to veto import restrictions on his product group! This manufacturer was able to sell his own product and our client's product through his already established network. The problem was solved.

Another company, one in pharmaceuticals, wanted to export to a

Middle East country. It heard that committee approval of the product was required. This would supposedly take two years. We shortened the cycle to two months instead of two years by having consultants assist.

Here's what happened. Prominent doctors in the country were visited by our consultant and told about the product. Then we sent government committee members carefully prepared information packages with all the material which was needed for approval. This included product data sheets, packaging and so on. Before the committee was due to meet, we asked if our client company could send a representative to attend the meetings.

The committee not only received the representative and listened to his story, but two of the committee members actually invited him to dinner at their homes! The approval cycle then took its normal channel with one exception. The consultancy intervention moved the file from the bottom to the top of the pile for consideration. It not only assured consideration, it cut a two-year waiting list.

Use determination as we did with this company. Even on the smallest issue, when encountering road blocks, look for alternatives.

Don't give up. Otherwise little obstacles lead to bigger ones. Remember the textile company which overcame import restrictions. Remember the pharmaceutical company which overcame the two-year wait on committee approval. If there's a will, there's a way.

Keeping your incentive in mind helps to increase your determination.

If you know the market potential—if you know what results you're aiming for—your priority will remain high. So will the company commitment to the project. This will carry you through the difficult times and keep you from abandoning the effort mid stream.

Third, follow it up as if it was your only market

This is the most common and the most heart-breaking of all reasons for failure. After thousands of dollars are spent on a trip abroad and after endless hours of preparation, the executive arrives home to a full desk of paperwork.

Unfortunately, the follow-up that needs to be done on the foreign market often loses out to other pressures. You can understand that the people overseas, not receiving the appropriate follow-up, presume interest has died. Then their interest and enthusiasm start to fade. I always say 'If you want to succeed in a foreign market, you must treat it as your *only* market.' Give it the attention it deserves.

'Out of sight, out of mind' applies to exporting more than most other things. No matter what country your dealing in, give it continuous attention.

Having local support of some kind has always proved to increase sales. Regardless of your industry or the country, you can engage local people, cost effectively, to keep things moving, to alert you to problems and to save you trips to the market place. The extra effort pays valuable dividends. There are many consultants like ourselves and others who can help you to motivate agents and keep your project alive.

Don't forget the human factor when you're dealing overseas. People in some countries expect to get to know you and need to be entertained. In other countries a straightforward, direct approach is the only way to succeed.

Whether you're choosing an agent or acquiring a company, the human factor is critical. Whoever you're sending abroad to follow up on business, needs to be the type who can adapt to each situation. The dynamic Sales and Marketing Director of a large company might be perfect for large-scale negotiations. Yet someone else could be more effective in third world countries. Yet another personality could be needed to interface with entrepreneurs during acquisition discussions. Put the right person on the right job.

Most of the points we've discussed here are sensible, workable principles. But as Samuel Coleridge said, 'Common sense in an uncommon degree is what the world calls wisdom.' Foreign marketing requires greater wisdom because of the greater parameters involved. If you want to add markets profitably, we suggest you get a start, work aggressively, and follow up closely. And of them all, don't neglect the plan. Without the right plan, the rest is fruitless.

Remember, to Succeed in Overseas Markets:

Consider all options, then give it undying determination

23

Finding the Right Agent—It's Like Finding a Needle in a Haystack

How not to proceed

January—month 1

In January, Colin Jones, who heads up his own company making food processing equipment, decided to export to the USA. He told his Sales Director, John Martin, to stop off there on his way back from another overseas trip to get a feel for the competition. He did that in May. After three days looking around the market at competitive equipment and prices he wrote up his findings and told Colin Jones that he felt there was a market for them.

May—month 5

Colin and John were happy that the market looked promising. Their next job was to find an agent. They remembered an agent who approached them at an exhibition last year and so in July they wrote to him to see if he would be willing to represent them. The agent wrote back with a positive response in early September so Colin and John flew over there in October for discussions.

October—month 10

They came home feeling optimistic. They hadn't agreed on an agency contract in writing because the agent wanted to do a market survey and John and Colin needed to finalize their own prices including delivery.

Four months passed and they heard nothing from the agent. Finally, when contacting him by telephone they found out that he was no longer interested. That was February.

March—month 15

By March, now 15 months after their decision to break into the market, they decided to broaden their net and examine several other agents before leaping at another one. However, in April they received a cable from a small contracting company referred by the first agent. This company said it could acquire orders quickly and asked for several quotations. John and Colin thought they had better have a first-hand look at the company and its customers, but to save costs only Bill flew over this time. They realized that he could easily handle it on his own.

June—month 17

Things looked promising, and they sent their first shipment over at cost to break into the market in June. The first new customers were acquired, the market was buoyant and Colin made preparations to increase his production capacity. That was June.

December—month 24

By December the story was different. They weren't hearing from the agent any more. Orders had stopped. Colin managed to find out that the company had changed into a different area of business and had not been servicing their products properly. That wouldn't help their reputation. They sat back reflecting on the time, energy and money spent and wondered where they had gone wrong.

Summary:

- 24 months elapsed
- 3 plane tickets, travel expenses
- 15 working days of managerial time away from home base
- ? managerial planning time (high)
- - shipment at cost
- 0 progress on market entry

That's the experience of Colin Jones and John Martin. The story is strikingly like that which we hear from companies day in and day out.

What went wrong

Why is it that Colin and John didn't have more structure in their method of finding a good agent? Perhaps it's the lack of seeing their incentive clearly. If they had determined that the market could account for a certain percentage growth in their company in 12 months, and had they set stage-by-stage sales targets, would they have perhaps not let so much time pass between communications?

Also, had their incentive been clear and their targets set, wouldn't they have put more effort into looking at several agents and not just gamble on the first person they thought of, the one they met at a trade stand? Maybe, maybe not.

Let's compare selecting an agent to hiring sales personnel. I'm always amazed that companies spend so much time and effort recruiting sales people for their home base, and so little time and effort recruiting overseas agents. Yet an overseas agent can do more to increase turnover by opening up the market of a whole country than a salesperson can do at home in a single territory.

When companies hire salespeople, they train them. They put together targets. They watch over them. Yet when they take on agents, their attitude is less committed. Then they wonder why they don't get commitment back!

Use a structured approach

If you want to find the right agent you have to use a structured approach. You can't gamble. You don't appoint an agent you pick up at an exhibition without checking their references any more than you would pick up hitch hikers along the road and appoint them as your sales reps at home base. The gamble may pay off once, but let's face it, the odds are against you.

How many agents do you need? The US market, for example, is said to have 10 times the buying power of the UK. That means that it's worth 10 countries the size of Britain. Yet many companies see the USA as a single market and give it comparatively little attention.

Several American companies we know have the same problem with Europe. It seems far away and it's easy to think of it as one place. If you appoint an agent for all of Europe, you'll find that the language and cultural differences make it difficult to sell across borders.

The way we advise companies to find agents is to use a structured approach. Just as in the last chapter, you want to examine your options.

This time the options relate to representation. Will your agent be an importer, a distributor, another manufacturer who will act as an agent, or what? Ask yourself. Who do they sell to now? What targets will they and you aim for together? What training will you give? How often will you see them?

All these things are important in finding the right agent. Use a structured approach, don't gamble. It's better to find out differences of opinion before the relationship begins than later. Will all or part of that person's time be allocated? How much time? Will the head of the company promote your product or will one of the junior staff? Will you divide the advertising budget between yourselves? How much? When and where will it be spent?

Perhaps it sounds like too much trouble. But successful companies operate this way. They treat export with as much care, or more, than the home market. And why not—the return can be proportionally greater!

How *to* proceed

Here's a company that did it right. You'll see a striking difference in its planning, timing management practices to the one above.

At the same time that Colin Jones decided to export to the USA, so did Andy Smith. Andy's company made similar equipment and was located near Colin's.

January—month 1

The month was January. Andy knew from his research that his products could meet the local requirements. If he could gain only 3% of the market he could reach his growth objective. He called in his Sales Director, Mike Northfield to make a plan with deadlines for each stage. They listed their goals as:

- Structured Market Entry
- Effective Use of Management Time
- Rapid Increase in Revenue—25% in 12 months
- Steady Controlled Growth—100% in 3 years

Andy emphasized to Mike that he wanted every avenue of representation to be explored, before deciding what type of agent to choose. He wanted Mike to look for companies with:

— well-established sales contacts in their field and a good reputation with users and suppliers and
— technical and service capability.

These companies could be any of the following three:

- Agents or importers
- Distributors
- Compatible manufacturers who could act as agents

Mike went back to his desk and thought about every way he could use to identify companies in these three categories. He made a list of all the trade associations, government departments, end users and his personal contacts who might be able to help him.

By the third week in January he had sent letters to these people asking for their recommendations on companies they felt were qualified to act as agents—such as importers, distributors and compatible manufacturers.

February—month 2

By February he had learned of many companies in the three categories. He contacted the heads of those companies by letter, stressing the *benefits* and *features* of his products. He listed his sales objectives and suggested ways his company could support their sales efforts if they became agents. He asked them to respond before the first of March with details of their company.

He took special effort to follow each letter up 10 days later with a phone call to prove his seriousness and to further entice the company. His second reason for calling was that he was able to glean his own impressions of the company from his calls—the way the phone was answered—the way messages were taken—the way his questions were answered.

April—month 4

He listed the companies in priority order by what he had heard about them and from them. In April, after agreeing his plan with Andy, he contacted the top six companies on his list to arrange to visit them from May 17 to 20.

May—month 5

Before flying over there, he and Andy took pricing decisions on how long they could hold the exchange rate at the current level. If they obtained orders they would buy currency forward and so they included these costs in their pricing policy.

They also included shipping door to door to make buying easy for the customer. Mike made up price lists in UK sterling amounts, because he knew people preferred to deal in their own currency. Also, he knew that having the converted price lists with him would help him to keep his mind on the people and the negotiations instead of the calculator.

He arranged his visits so as to see the least likely company first. This would help him to become familiar with the industry and the way it operates in the UK, and would also give him preparation for going into meetings with the most likely candidates. It would also allow him to practise his own presentation and to see how to refine his package to meet the local needs. He remembered that the Americans are straightforward in their approach so he carefully planned to make his benefits and targets clear from the beginning of his discussions.

The meetings went well and on the third day he came to a full working agreement with one of the companies to import his product, and later to manufacture it under licence if the sales targets were reached. The manufacturing option would also protect Andy and Mike if the exchange rate went against them.

Mike made a second visit the following day to iron out the first order details, the sales targets, the training, literature and the dates that each would carry out the actions. They put their joint commitments on paper.

The head of the company told Mike he was impressed with his efficiency. He said he liked to deal with companies who were organized from the beginning because they always performed better later. Then he told Mike of another foreign supplier he'd dealt with in the past who didn't keep to his commitments. He didn't want to get burnt twice.

There was a lot of work involved in securing orders and it was a disappointment to have suppliers let you down. He almost refused to see Mike, in fact, but his efficiency and persistence throughout had told him to take a second chance. Now he was glad he had. He was sure their working relationship would be mutually profitable.

On the fourth evening Mike boarded the plane to go home with an agency agreement in his pocket and satisfaction that his preparation had paid off. In addition he had an order worth 15% of his first year's target. But the order wasn't the end of the road. He knew Andy wanted steady, controlled growth and he knew he had found the right company to support their efforts for their three-year, 100% growth plan.

It had been an exhausting trip. It was a tempting thought to put all the paperwork away during the flight and catch a little sleep, but he knew his desk would be piled up with new demands on his first day back. He knew he'd better write his follow-up report, letters, plan of action and commitments now while his notes were fresh in his mind.

He remembered hearing that we forget 80% of what we hear after two days, and so even though he had clear notes, he decided he'd better do it now while it was fresh in his mind. Then his follow-up points could be actioned on his first day back. That would move them closer to the 100% growth plan.

As his plane approached home he reflected on what a good feeling it was to work for a company which set specific growth plans. 'When you make a contribution here, you know exactly how it fits into the total plan,' he thought to himself. He knew Andy would be ecstatic with his results and give him recognition for his achievement.

Summary:
5   months elapsed
1   plane ticket, travel expenses
4   working days of management time away from home base
−   managerial planning time (effective)
+   shipment with profit
+   progress on market entry (order worth 15% of first year's growth
    target)

That's the experience of Andy Smith and Mike Northfield. The successful mode of operation is the same in all companies we work with who pursue profit seriously.

During this session of our Develop Effective Sales seminars, we sometimes have people say they wish they had a Mike Northfield working for them. Others say they wish they had an Andy Smith as a boss! These kinds of people do exist. We know them and work with them.

Peter Blandford in England is a case in point. He handles the export for DRG stationery. The DRG group is Europe's largest supplier of stationery and the world's largest supplier of envelopes. Peter has been known to stay up all night if necessary to get the terms of agreement right and to secure the order before flying out.

He knows he can do business personally, and that leaving without the order makes it as good as lost. The Group Managing Director, Ian Lawrie, sets a good example himself. I've known Ian for some time and know he's not adverse to working weekends either here or abroad. He sets the example. No wonder DRG has been on England's list of top 100 exporters.

Fumi Nakagome in Japan is another case in point. She knows how important the personal contact is to getting business. Her philosophy is,

'Never write when you can call, and never call when you can visit.' She should know, she's been running the International Inspection Company in Tokyo as President for many years and has worked for three prime ministers in Japan as adviser on various issues.

If we want to find the right agent we have to get out there and look. We have to visit them and be sure we're taking the right decision.

Finding the right agent is like finding a needle in the hay-stack, not because they don't exist, but because companies don't know how to look for them. They gamble on the first one that comes along rather than to use a structured approach like Mike Northfield. They take the easy road, only to find out later that they've wasted their time, money and effort.

Effort is the keynote. I know from my own experience that searching for agents is one of business's most exhausting exercises— if done right. On my most recent trip to Egypt, I had 24 appointments spread over seven days in Cairo and Alexandria. Even with the support of local consultants, and with knowing the country quite well, I always find that the constant negotiation, meetings and decision-making takes its toll by the end of the trip.

Doing business successfully in an environment of uncertainty is almost impossible. Get advice from others who have succeeded. Bob Northfield didn't jump on a plane the minute Andy mentioned England. He contacted everyone he thought of who could help. He did it quickly and effectively.

All the planning and preparation and you can do ahead will pay off. This is true of each and every country. Remember the two years wasted by Colin Jones and Bill Martin. Don't let it happen to you.

Remember, to Succeed in Overseas Markets:

Use a Structural Approach, Don't Gamble

24

Wake up to Cultural Pitfalls—In Presentation, In Negotiations, In Follow-Up

On one of my trips to Egypt, I was in the procurement offices of the Egyptian National Railroad. I had an appointment with the Director of the department, and when I went into the office, as so often happens in Egypt, there were several meetings going on at the same time. Over on one side of his very large room were four young Japanese gentlemen, with blueprints spread all over the table. They were casually dressed, well entrenched in their conversation and clearly planning to stay for some time.

I returned the next day to see the Director again with some additional information, and they were still there. I had the impression that they planned to stay for days or weeks.

I forgot about the situation until, some trips later, I heard talk of the new high-speed train to Alexandria. A friend advised me to take it because was quicker than flying or driving—and the latest thing in Cairo. Everyone was talking about it.

When I arrived at the platform, the new train pulled in, and spread all across the side was a beautiful large Japanese symbol. Yes, of course, it clicked. I'd forgotten—the Japanese had won that contract—they had stayed and negotiated as long as it took to win.

Understand the competitor's business style

When we're dealing in foreign markets, we must remember that the competition will be fierce. We have many cultural differences to be aware of—not just the customer, but also the competitor.

I know another Japanese salesman who was sent to the Middle East to win a contract. He's been there eight months and comes back and forth to England occasionally for a short break. But he won't go home until he wins.

Colin Marshall of British Airways recently addressed a function I attended. Colin has built an excellent reputation at Avis in the USA and later with British Airways in the UK. He was warning English executives to beware of the American business ethic—to win is everything, unlike the British who value the sport.

Yet how many of us would be prepared to stay abroad until we won?

Prince Charles was in the news in late 1985 for his controversial statements about English business. He had just returned from his trip to America and saw the comparisons in business style. It left him with the fear that, unless changes were made, Britain could become a fourth-rate nation. 'We do need a sense of urgency in our outlook about business,' he was quoted as saying.

The day is gone when we can insulate ourselves from the outside world. I can get to Japan, a third of the way around the world, in less time than it took my grandparents to travel by horse and buggy from Prague to their home in an outlying village. The world is closing in on us. The cultural differences are much more important now.

Understand the customer's business style

If we step over the threshold into a new market place, the cultural differences are up to us to overcome. We have to play according to their rules.

By their rules, I mean the buyers. But the story doesn't end there. We have another set of rules to pay attention to as well—that of the competitors! So there are only two sets of cultural differences to pay attention to. That's not so bad if we do our homework right, if we're adaptable, flexible and talented.

That reminds me of a comment made by Kenneth Minton of Laporte Industries which had acquired several private American companies. Together these small companies amounted to 100 million US dollars. One piece of advice he has for companies serious about acquisitions is to send someone from the parent company to negotiations who understands entrepreneurs. Doesn't that make sense for every business venture? Send someone who understand the players. Otherwise you lose the game. It's important in presentation, in negotiations and in follow-up.

I remember one client who went to the Middle East without

understanding the importance of building up a social rapport with customers and agents. He had a difficult product line, one that was very price conscious, and our job—to find him an agent—was not an easy one.

During an interview, one agent casually invited everyone to lunch. The client refused the invitation. Naturally the agent was insulted.

Little did our client know that his chances of getting local representation were going down by the minute. Luckily our project manager who accompanied him from London saved the day by unobtrusively taking the client aside, explaining the situation, and turning the lunch decision around.

There you have it. A difficult product, in a difficult market. You manage to find an agent, which is like finding a needle in a haystack and the whole market is almost lost at the negotiation stage by a lack of cultural understanding.

One of America's biggest defence contractors recently sent a marketing man over from head office to present his case to the European ministries. This person had never before set foot outside American soil. His management style was untampered by European influence. They perceived him as arrogant and aggressive. His style wasn't tuned in to the British way of doing things. He hadn't taken the time to consult others to find out who the key players were, or find out about their needs and personalities.

After half a day of meetings, the British threw him out on his ear, so he flew across the channel to upset the French.

Did he win either contract? No.

Was the contract important to the company? Yes.

Did the marketing man do his homework by first contacting his firm's overseas employees to get their advice or their technical input? No.

Why not? You tell us. Perhaps it was pride, perhaps politics, perhaps ignorance.

It's 'people' who make or break business, not necessarily the product or the price. Bill and I see it every day. Companies spend hours, days, weeks and months reducing their prices and talking about better products development. Then they send the wrong, or an untrained, person over to the market place to represent them. The sale is lost the minute that person steps off the airplane.

Adapt your methods to suit the culture

Figure 12 shows the pitfalls most often seen in overseas selling. The four categories represent our segments of the sales process—preparation, presentation, negotiation and follow-up.

Of all the segments, presentation and follow-up are the two in which most companies fall down on when trying to do business in a foreign culture. Let's look at each segment to find ways of overcoming the pitfalls.

Pitfall A— Preparation

The company fails to choose the right country for its product, or the right agent or entry mode.

Don't pick the country or agent for reason of ease rather than investigation. *Make sure* your product is right for the market, know if the market size is large enough to warrant your effort, speak the language, be sure you can service the marketplace, learn about cultural difference and be sure your people can adapt.

Pitfall B—Presentation

The content or style of the presentation is wrong for the marketplace.

Don't fail to adapt your presentation to local demands and customs— remember the American who lost the European contracts. *Make sure* that your presentation material meets local standards, that the person doing the presentation will be accepted, that your pace of aggressiveness is right for the market, that you tell the benefits and features which are important locally.

Pitfall C—Negotiation

After convincing the buyers of the product's features, benefits, price and quality, the company fails to convince on secondary issues.

Secondary issues could be faith in delivery, quality control, management trust, long-term relationship building, etc. *Make sure*—remember you're selling to emotional needs as well as factual—they need to trust you/like dealing with you/see long-term benefits developing.

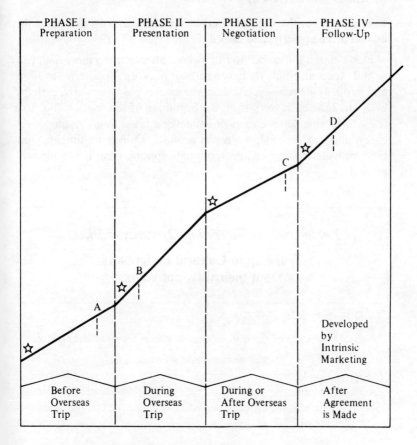

A = Company fails in the right country to select agent or entry mode.
B = Presentation style or content wrong for marketplace.
C = After convincing the buyer of the product's features, benefits, and quality, the company fails to convince on secondary issues
D = Even after positive decision is made, company fails to support marketplace properly and sales dwindle.
☆ = Critical action required.

¦ = Pitfall areas likely to result in lost business.

Figure 12   The pitfalls most often seen in overseas selling

Pitfall D—Follow-Up

Even after a positive decision is made, the company fails to support the market place properly, and sales dwindle.

Don't expect the market to run without attention any more than you would expect an employee to run without back-up support, motivation and so on. *Make sure*—you contact the market place regularly, perhaps even one time each week from the beginning of the relationship. Use telex, telephone, letters, visits or whatever it takes to get results. Send everything you promise, when you promise. Deliver on time, pay on time, provide training and promotional support. Treat it as your *only* market.

Remember, to Succeed in Overseas Markets:

**Wake up to Cultural Differences
Do it their way, not yours.**

Review of Part Seven

Successes and Failures in Overseas Markets

Chapter 22   How to Plan Your Entry for Maximum Results

1. First, Plan Carefully Considering All Options
2. Second, Implement the Plan Going Around the Roadblocks
3. Third, Follow it up as if it Was Your Only Market

Chapter 23   Finding the Right Agent—It's Like Finding a Needle in the Haystack

1. Use a Structured Approach
2. Don't Gamble

Chapter 24   Wake Up to Cultural Differences—in Presentations, in Negotiating, in Follow-Up

1. Understanding the Competitor's Business Style
2. Understand the Customer's Business Style
2. Adapt Your Methods to Suit the Culture

Part VII Action Sheet

Ideas for Development:

- Consider all market entry options
- Use a structured approach. Don't gamble
- Wake up to cultural differences. Do it their way, not yours
-
-
-
-
-

Of the above ideas, which one is likely to yield the best results?

What percentage of sales (or performance) increase could realistically be expected?

How long would it take:
   to develop the idea?
   to get results?

Who would have to be involved?

What date should we start?

What is the first step I should take?

Consolidating Your Forward Plan

25

Responsible—Who, me?

In the mid 1700s, Samuel Johnson, the great English writer from Lichfield, said, 'To do nothing is in everyone's power!'

Mark Twain said 'It ain't those parts of the Bible that I can't understand that bother me, it's the parts I do understand.'

We often understand what needs to be done in life if we're honest with ourselves, but being the humans that we are, we let obstacles stand in our way.

I remember listening to Harry Browne, the radical, self-proclaimed economist, author and lecturer, who predicted the American bank collapses of recent years. Someone asked him how, since he had no formal training in economics, he could predict these events. 'These are all obvious,' he said. 'You need only sit quietly under an apple tree and reflect on the facts.'

And so it is for all of us. We know, when we take time to reflect on it, what needs to be done in our life, our business, our personal relationships. Yet we let obstacles stand in the way. We delay. We procrastinate. We make excuses to ourselves. That's human, perhaps. Yet we see that the great achievers reflect on these human failings and take action against them.

Ben Franklin dedicated much of his life overcoming what he thought were his personality defects. In his autobiography, printed in 1868, he outlined 13 virtues he pursued each day of the week.

This pursuit didn't stop all the other things that he did. It didn't stop him from inventing, from politicking, from influencing world events for years to come. He took the time to take responsibility for everything he wanted to achieve in life.

There are pages of proven techniques in this book which if implemented will reap tremendous results. Results which can transform lives and companies. Yet, nothing will happen if we, ourselves, don't take responsibility for implementing them.

Over the years, I've worked with almost every imaginable industry. I worked with manufacturers, with service companies, with financiers, with retailers etc. I've helped them to sell better, to motivate, to plan their future and to export. I know their companies backward and forwards.

I could talk about business improvement techniques for weeks and months. But I haven't. In working with Bill Sykes, we've picked out only 25 areas of concentration for you, which we know apply to *all* businesses and organizations. These 25 areas have been tried and tested with our private clients and with hundreds and hundreds of companies at our public and in-house business development seminars. They've been tried and tested with all levels of people – company presidents and junior personnel – in the USA, in England, in Athens, in Brussels, in Singapore, in Tokyo.

Even with all this evidence a few managers from time to time enter our seminars with hesitation. They use a sceptical approach, looking for reasons things won't work. And that's valid to a point. But if you are that type of person by nature, don't let your scepticism stop you from advancing. You'll always find reasons things won't work and reasons things will work.

It's up to you to focus on the positive. It's up to you to make things happen.

I like what Christopher Morley said about success. 'There is only one success, and that is to be able to spend your life in your own way.'

What specific things do you want to achieve in life? How do you want to spend it? Ben Franklin knew it wasn't easy to have everything perfect, so he got a start on it by taking one step at a time. He kept at it. He achieved what he wanted.

As you've read throught this book, you've probably had a lot of ideas about how you could relate the principles to your own situation to get the success you want. Which one will you start on first?

Start small and build steadily

Our advice is to start small. Choose a principle that you can visualize implementing easily. Choose one that will bring results quickly. Then build on it.

Remember our management trainees who recorded two things per day which they achieved? This reinforced the fact that they were making progress. It got results.

If you choose an achievable principle, you'll get results and you'll continue to build. You can refer back to the principles in the book often to continue your building process.

If you choose an overwhelming set of principles which require too much time out of your already busy schedule, they'll die a death, and perhaps never recover. Yes, starting small and building step by step is essential to success.

That doesn't mean your goals should be small. The big picture is made up of component parts. Remember the section on management controls? We said that it was important to analyse results in specific segments. The same is true with carrying out your forward plan. Take it segment by segment. When you consolidate all the segments, you'll have reached your goal.

It's not possible to follow up everything we start, but if we want success, we need undying persistence on the things that matter most to us.

We can all think of a lot of reasons to abandon our golden rule of 'strict follow-up'.

Nobody said it's easy. You have to have a sharp focus on the light at the end of the tunnel and compare it constantly to your alternative, which is usually not achieving anything. It's easy to abandon our goal, but later it's a disappointing feeling.

Foster responsibility

If we want to achieve our goals, other people will be important. How will we keep them motivated to take responsibility—to overcome the obstacles which stand in the way?

Ian McCallum, our friend who heads Critchley, the makers of conduits and cable markers, has a technique which is very effective. Ian, like other successful directors we know, has an appetite for new ideas. He prepares himself by trying new ideas and absorbing them in his working style. What better way is there to motivate employees than to set an example!

I met Ian one day at Heathrow airport near our Brentford office on his return flight from Europe. He said he had learned a very good management technique from dealing with my company.

At our first meeting, he said, our project manager, Angus Garfield, had gone through a pro-forma of what we had expected from that meeting—a list of points we hoped to cover. Ian felt that was a very effective way to begin a meeting and had used it in Europe—leading his customer through a point-by-point agenda of terms. The result was immensely successful and Ian was determined to use it in all future meetings.

Ian believes that people look to their boss for ideas, and how right he is. If the boss is willing to take responsibility for better ways of doing things, it sets an example for all. If we want to instill responsibility in others, shouldn't we show them the way?

Angus Garfield, who gave Ian this idea, was a person who always commanded the respect of clients several years his senior. Angus knew his areas of strength and pursued them. What was his major strength? Enthusiasm.

Whenever anyone at the office missed their targets or had a bad day, Angus was the first to say 'Cheer up, tomorrow will bring success.' He was always the one to congratulate people for doing a job well. 'You really handled that well,' he'd say.

No wonder Ian liked his approach to the point-by-point agenda.

Would he have liked Angus's methods if Angus had presented the idea without the right attitude? Without enthusiasm? Probably not.

Angus commanded leadership. He took responsibility by using his best asset—enthusiasm. What are the best assets of your people? Find them and you'll find the key to fostering responsibility.

Training is another important part of preparing ourselves and others for responsibility. Itsu Yamamoto, the dynamic president of the Eico Company in Tokyo, told me that training a person for management is no different than training a part of the body. When we learn to throw a ball, the arm learns to move efficiently in a certain way, just as the legs learn to walk.

And so it is in management. Training, he says, is an ongoing process. Itsu meets his people on a regular basis. He expects them to learn his philosophy as well as the practices of the company.

In his business of importing products and selling to the Japanese market, there must be a trust built up between himself and his customer. Therefore every detail must be known to employees dealing with an account. Mr Yamamoto wants his people to take responsibility and so he gives them the skill they need.

What other steps can we take to overcome that obstacle of responsibility? I particularly like the philosophy that retired Coach John Wooden of UCLA taught his award-winning basketball teams who won national championships, year after year: 'I will get ready, and then perhaps my chance will come.' Should we take responsibility for our own training or should we wait for others to prepare us? We know what Coach Wooden would say. The fact is that it's up to us to get ready.

Reinforce everyone's distinctive competence

Jim Kearns goes by the 'Distinctive Competence' doctrine. He gets to know his people well, in order to help them identify their distinctive competence. 'Do better what you do best' is one of Jim's mottos. Despite heavy travel commitments Jim takes time to get to know his people. He helps them recognize their distinctive competence. When they know what they're best at, they take responsibility.

The same was true of the management trainees. As they recorded two successes per day they gained an understanding of their ability. They reinforced their ability to succeed.

Do whatever it takes for you to succeed. Talk to yourself, Make notes to remind yourself. Listen to your principles on a cassette as you drive to work. Do whatever it takes for you to keep on course. Take Morley's advice and set your forward plan and work step by step to achieve your success and to spend your life in your own way.

Remember, to Consolidate your Forward Plan:

Start with achievable principles and build on them relentlessly. Keep your mind focused on the results and the benefits you'll gain.

Review of Part Eight

Consolidating
Your Forward Plan

Chapter 25   Responsible—Who, me?

1. Start Small and Build Steadily
2. Foster Responsibility
3. Reinforce Everyone's Distinctive Competence

Part VIII Action Sheet

Ideas for Development:

- Choose achievable goals and build relentlessly
- Keep the mind focused on the results and the benefits to be gained
-

-

-

-

-

-

Of the above ideas, which one is likely to yield the best results?

What percentage of sales (or performance) increase could realistically be expected?

How long would it take:
  to develop the idea?
  to get results?

Who would have to be involved?

What date should we start?

What is the first step I should take?

Acknowledgements

'Good morning, America' is a phrase I often use when calling Bill in Baltimore. It's ironic to hear his British accent coming across the phone line as I speak with my fellow Americans from London. The jesting we give each other for living in reciprocal countries—the second sense we have for Anglo-American situations—has produced a working relationship which is extremely rewarding. It has eased the burden of writing a book with an ocean between us, of collaborating on seminars and consulting projects—all tasks which would be impossible without that bond and dedication to make the impossible happen.

The key facilitators in all of this have been our spouses, Angela Sykes and Tom Harvey, whose supportive, enthusiastic and positive attitude is a driving force to all who know them. The effect of their support is boundless and I can't find words to describe it.

A special thanks goes to all of our management trainees—Josef Rutzel and Barbara Bohm, from Germany, Amy Barad and Angus Garfield from America, who gave special input to the early days at Intrinsic Marketing, as well as Melissa Alonso, Brian Napack, David Burwick, Christine Bischoff, Claudia Krippner, Frank Leippert and many others whose friendship and dedication I will always value.

Many other people have added to the quality of life and inspiration of ideas. These include people in India, Egypt, Japan, Europe and America I've had the pleasure of meeting through my association with Zonta, the international business women's organization, through the British Association of Women Entrepreneurs, Network, and in England through the London Chamber of Commerce and Industry and the Institute of Directors.

Bill and I are extremely grateful to the friends and clients quoted in the book for their continuing support. In addition my special thanks goes to Derek Coltman, Education Director, at the Institute of Directors, whose support and friendship has helped to make our seminars a success and to my Most Promising Young Business Woman award recipients, Judith Leeming, Susan McAll, Sue Hall, Fiona Greenwood, Ruth Dunlop, Julie McLeod and Helen Powell who have been sheer delights to work with.

To Anne Joelle Galley who helped us build the skeleton of the 'Develop Effective Sales' seminars and who proof read the manuscript while in Switzerland, Mexico and inflight around the world. To my family—Darrin, Laurie and Tom for their support and to my husband who sacrificed countless days and evenings of our life together last winter while the book was being produced, for his honesty, support and final hour proof reading.

To Ana Maria Miranda who, while here from Chile, gave long hours and dedication producing the manuscript to perfection and to the special people over the years without whom life would not be the same—Hilde Bartlett, JP, for her loyal friendship, Walter Blackburn of Dale Carnegie Associates for his genuine support, and from Bill to Walter Goldsmith whose management style influence was invaluable during Bill's days at Black and Decker.

Finally special thanks goes to our literary agent, Frances Kelly, whose efforts and talent made this book and its many translations possible—German, French, Dutch, Swedish, Greek and Japanese— and to the people at Kogan Page, whose sincere help have made the publishing experience memorable and rewarding. Thank you all.

Index

A Profit in
Her Own Time

The following is reproduced from Peak Magazine, Hong Kong.

For the world to beat a path to your door, it was once enough simply to build a better mousetrap. Not any more. Now you must spell out not only why your product is better, but also just how it will benefit those who buy it. And if you can publish your message in paperback form and make a killing out of that, even better. *Your Pursuit Of Profit* is the latest addition to the fast-growing body of literature on the subject of business: the cardinal do's and don'ts and, of course, how to propel your sales through the roof.

Co-authored by Christine Harvey and Bill Sykes, the book already looks poised to overtake some of its best-known predecessors, such as *The One-Minute Manager* and *In Pursuit of Excellence*. In its first month it achieved 360% of its target sales in London; German, French and Flemish translation rights were sold and Japanese translation rights were on the way.

Christine Harvey, who visited Hong Kong and Japan earlier this year to promote the publication and hold seminars for management organizations, has a simple explanation for the runaway success of the book. As someone who has been involved in sales all her life, and has managed three thriving businesses of her own, she knows her subject. What she writes is based on her personal experience: input from her years of business consulting and the 'Develop Successful Sales' seminars she founded with British-born American resident, Bill Sykes.

Harvey's business life began in her native California when she took a junior counter-sales job to pay her way through college. The selling bug bit, and rungs on the career ladder included corporate positions at AT & T. Seven years ago, she set up her highly successful consultancy, Intrinsic Marketing. 'I had to sell the consulting service. Any time you start your own business there's a very strong sales element. You may have the best product in the world but it doesn't sell itself.

'Regardless of what you are selling, you have to identify your customer base, and then you have to learn how to put across the benefits of the product or service in a way that people can understand.' The importance of outlining the advantages of consumer items is one area which *Your Pursuit Of Profit* looks at, though this is far from a new concept, Harvey explained. During her stay in Japan, she found a book on the teachings of Buddha in a hotel room. 'There it was, an age-old philosophy saying the same thing about benefits. Buddha tells the story of a man who returns home to find his house on fire, with his children inside. He calls them to come out: "Quick, quick, you're in danger." But the children do not even hear him. He tries again: "Children, come out quickly, I have some presents for you," and this time they hear him and come out. They were offered a benefit which was important to them and they were willing to act.

'I am sometimes asked why companies fail. In my experience, it is not because of the product. People who start companies think that all they need is a unique idea or a fantastic product. They go through a lot of research and development without having any idea of how to start selling it. People lose business needlessly because they don't move during the peak interest period. Somebody buying a lipstick or piece of costume jewellery probably has no more than a three-minute attention span. But buying aerospace equipment, it could be three years.'

In lectures to large companies such as computer giant IBM, Harvey frequently reminds her audiences about employee motivation, another area examined in the book (pertinently subtitled: 'Motivate yourself and others to develop effective sales'). 'The key to motivation is to find out what the employee needs, and then respond appropriately. Too many managers presume that all salespeople are motivated by money. They build in incentives which are financial and they forget to support individual human needs. Salespeople need a lot of positive reinforcement.'

How does Harvey deal with the problem of trying to get her message across to people of different cultural backgrounds? Of *Your Pursuit Of Profit*, she says: 'We've chosen twenty-five areas that have proved to be in need of improvement in every company, everywhere. You must be aware of cultural differences, but people make too much of them. What we need to start doing is to look at the similarities. In every country, people have their own ideas, motivations and desires. That's what makes business tick: it's people.'

North America is generally regarded as the most go-ahead business environment. Nevertheless, in 1976, Harvey and her husband, Tom, settled in England. 'It was a personal decision. My husband and I had travelled to England several times, like the English people very much and wanted a cultural change. It took us about twelve years of planning to get there, but we have no regrets—apart from the weather.' (Harvey catches up on her tan on frequent visits back to her native California.) She also remains unimpressed by the sluggish British business scene.

'People often ask why I feel Britain is moving backwards: at the beginning of the nineteenth century, the country had 90% of world trade; by 1950 it was 50%; today it is only a small fraction. It's obvious that competition is growing around the world, but the Europeans are losing track of it. And there's a danger for European companies of resting on their laurels. Asian countries are moving ahead very quickly; there's a determination in Asia, and a speed of doing things that is impossible in Europe or America. Asia generally has a responsiveness to the needs of the customer that is second to none.

'Asians also have to watch out that they don't become complacent in some areas. Tourism is very important in Asia, with large numbers of business travellers. Reputations spread around the world fast and a hotel that has a fabulous reputation can quickly lose it if the staff become arrogant and complacent. In this fast-moving environment you can't afford to take anything for granted.

Harvey is delighted by the paperback's progress to date. 'It's a marvellous feeling, because when you write a book you put your heart and soul into it. People often ask about the sequel, but I'm against authors who come out with a second book just for the sake of it. What I'm concentrating on is getting the message across. People need workable methods to increase their effectiveness in life, in the community and in their business. We tried to show how a 10% change can get 100% better results.'

Books and business-school theories have a very real place in today's commercial world, Christine Harvey believes. 'You've got to start somewhere. If you don't know anything about production, you have to read about it, talk about it, look at it. You have to start with some techniques such as those you learn in business school. But my advice would be to keep an open mind about them, don't take them as gospel, and remember they need to be tempered with the human factor.'

JANE RAM

To apply even more ...

If you want to learn even more you may be interested in the 'Pursuit of Profit' Seminars which are held by Christine Harvey and Bill Sykes throughout the year in various worldwide locations. Participants use a specially designed course manual and action plans which they each relate directly to their own situation. This enables them to project the results achievable from each segment of the course, prioritize the actions, and plan each step needed to achieve the desired results. To find out more about dates and locations ...

For Europe, the Middle East, the Far East contact:

Christine Harvey
Develop Effective Sales Seminars
Intrinsic Marketing
Blandford House
65 Blandford Street
London, England
W1H 3AJ
Telephone: (London) 01 486 8233
Telex: 299067, FAX: 935-0896

For USA and Canada

Bill Sykes
Develop Effective Sales Seminars
Sykes Consultants
Suite 800
Inner Harbo. Center
400 East Pratt Street
Baltimore, Maryland
U.S.A. 21202
Telephone: 301-576-8971
Telex: 87681 HQ BAL, FAX: 301-727-5250

Please send me more information about the dates of 'Pursuit of Profit' Seminars and the location nearest me:

Name ....

Full Address ....
(with company name if relevant)

....

Country .... Post Code ....

Telephone/Telex/Fax (optional) ....

Your Pursuit of Profit

Erratum – page 146

A CHECKLIST FOR CHAPTER 17

A Checklist for Evaluating Effective Sales Presentations

Points to check (for myself and other members of staff)	Level of proficiency (1–10)	Needs training (Yes/No)	Ways we can support others and train ourselves

• Prepared ahead
  – papers
  – examples
  – demonstrations			

• Knows product			
• Presents features			
• Presents benefits			
• Finds out which benefit the customer wants – 'Dominant Buying Motive'			
• Tells only important benefits			
• Handles fear vs confidence on objectives			
• Can make point in two minutes on phone			
• Can make point in 17 minutes in person			
• Recognizes emotional needs of customer			
• Recognizes logical needs of customer			
• Follows up on time			
• Has a follow-up system of control			
• Gets commitments			
• Asks for orders